TRANSFIGURATION

Introduction to the Contemplation of Icons

by Maria Giovanna Muzj

translated by Kenneth D. Whitehead

introduction by Fr. Egon Sendler

St. Paul Books & Media

Library of Congress Cataloging-in-Publication Data

Muzj, Maria Giovanna, 1945–
    [Trasfigurazione. English]
    Transfiguration: introduction to the contemplation of icons / by Maria
Giovanna Muzj : translated by Kenneth D. Whitehead.
        p. cm.
    Translation of: Trasfigurazione.
    Includes bibliographical references.
    ISBN 0-8198-7350-0 :
    1. Icons—Cult.   2. Orthodox Eastern Church—Doctrines.   3. Catholic
Church—Cult.   I. Title.
  BX323.M6813   1991
  246'.53—dc20   91-2341
                                                                           CIP

ISBN 0-8198-7350-0

All scriptural quotes are taken from the *New Jerusalem Bible,* Copyright © 1985
by Darton, Longman & Todd, Ltd., and Doubleday & Company, Inc. Reprinted
by permission of the publisher.

Original Title: *Trasfigurazione: Introduzione alla contemplazione delle icone*
© Figlie di S. Paolo, 1987.

Illustrations provided through the kindness of the Center "Russia Ecumenica" of
Rome, Italy; *Conception of St. Anne,* through the kindness of Ikonenmuseum,
Recklinghausen, Germany.

Printed and published in the U.S.A. by St. Paul Books & Media
50 St. Paul's Avenue, Boston, MA 02130.

St. Paul Books & Media is the publishing house of the Daughters of St. Paul, an
international congregation of women religious serving the Church with the com-
munications media.

1 2 3 4 5 6 7 8 9   99 98 97 96 95 94 93 92 91

Contents

Publications on icons are becoming more numerous. For the most part, however, they are either technical works, or else they are merely content to present some examples of the most beautiful iconographic productions of the Eastern Church, remaining on a rather superficial level. This book proposes to present iconographic art in its own right, inserting it into the theological and spiritual history of the Christian East, studying its laws of composition and artistic realization, and finally, guiding the reader towards a discovery of the profound meaning of these sacred representations which belong not only to the liturgy and worship of the Eastern Churches but also to the spirituality of the whole Christian people. The author has succeeded in making her attentive readers participate in these great riches. Although forming a united whole, the commentaries on the individual icons can be used separately, either as a point of departure for prayer and reflection or as an outline for catechesis.

Maria Giovanna Muzj was born in 1945. She took her university degree in literature and then dedicated herself to the study of theology (MA in theology) and, in particular, Eastern theology. Her thesis in religious studies was published under the title *The Eucharistic Prayer;* in this work she compared the Eastern and Western traditions. She has gone on to study iconography in depth from the viewpoints of both aesthetics and theology. Characteristically, her thought is not restricted to only one aspect of this vast field; she is particularly concerned with the theological and spiritual message of art.

In addition to teaching at the Pontifical Gregorian University in Rome, Ms. Muzj has given numerous lectures on the subject of iconography. *Transfiguration* is the fruit of her labors in this field. Reading and meditating upon the excellent reproductions of icons in this volume and upon the accompanying texts, the reader will be impressed by the rich message icons convey and may discover a compelling need to further contemplate the iconographical art.

Introduction

This volume proposes to introduce the reader to the contemplation of sacred icons. Contemplation should not be confused with simple artistic appreciation. It involves a great deal more than that. Indeed, it involves an exercise of living faith in Jesus Christ, who came to reveal the Father to us.

We should not be surprised, therefore, if the commentary that accompanies the presentation of this collection of icons—which includes some of the most beautiful and significant of all icons—contains as many historical references as it contains analyses of the structural and aesthetic qualities of each icon. In general, the tradition of the West may be able to consider the aesthetic qualities of religious images apart from the content of the faith which inspired them; but the same cannot be said for the tradition of the art of iconography itself. For the latter is more than a mere testimony of faith; it is also a kind of proclamation of the mystery of salvation itself. It is therefore fitting that we become aware of all the components of this art form.

It is especially necessary to keep returning to the theological content that the iconographer was always striving to present to Christian believers in order to assist them in developing their own faith and prayer. Unless we keep this theological perspective constantly in mind, we run the risk of remaining on the surface of things without delving into the true meanings the icons represent. We run the risk of being preoccupied merely with colors and forms.

The icon is even more an image for the eyes of faith than for the eyes of the flesh. The icon strives to be an image of what is invisible; it aims to teach the faith. The icon is always under a double obligation of fidelity: it must be faithful to our world, which was created by God; it must also be faithful to that same God, who can neither be circumscribed nor reduced to a representation. With earthly means—form, color, light—the icon must represent the religious reality of the world beyond this visible world. Since its object is beyond the visible world, it must be guided not primarily by aesthetic imperatives but rather by faith and revelation. This is what constitutes the double obligation that inspires the art of iconography. If we forget this, we run the risk of never being able to enter into the world of icons and of reducing the icon to a simple "religious picture," or even to some kind of aesthetic idol.

The contemplation of sacred icons in the theological sense is very different from the appreciation of religious images or representations in the West. However, we must observe that the fundamental theology of icons was defined by the Second Council of Nicaea in 787 and is common to the entire Church. This iconology forms an integral part of the Catholic faith, as has been confirmed by other councils. However, it has not been developed and integrated into the life of the Latin Church as it has been in the Greek Orthodox and other Eastern Churches.

The reasons for this may well reside in the particular spirituality of the West, in which the Word of God and the structure of the faith receive greater emphasis than its artistic expression. Another reason may be that the West was not confronted to the same degree with the typical Eastern heresies of a monophysite tendency.

The authentic theological conception of icons was worked out in the course of the crisis of iconoclasm in the eighth and ninth centuries. The crisis shook Byzantine culture to its roots and had an enormous effect on the political and economic life of the times as well. Not only were images as figurative representations called into question; the very dogma of the Incarnation, an essential element of the Christian faith, was also challenged.

10

At the center of the discussion was the image, or icon, of Christ himself. Defenders of images declared that it was not only the divinity of Christ that was manifested in the icon, since divinity stands above and beyond any possible art form or human language. Nor was the icon merely a picture of Jesus of Nazareth. No, the icon aimed to represent the person (hypostasis) of Christ in its integrity; that is to say, the mysterious union in the Word of the divine nature with a human nature.

The icon is thus a reflection of the Incarnation; it represents a presence. The reality of the prototype is present in the reality of the image. Between these two realities is the link which constitutes the likeness or resemblance, according to one of the greatest theologians of the icon, St. Theodore the Studite. This likeness is of the spiritual order and is accessible to the human intelligence. This may appear surprising and perhaps rationalistic, but it is not a question of a purely human intelligence. On that level, the icon would in truth be nothing but a simple object of art. The likeness in question, therefore, is not to be understood in any purely naturalistic fashion. Rather, it is to be understood as a kind of epiphany which unfolds before the soul enlightened by faith. The icon reaches beyond the mere natural faculties of the human spirit and discloses its total meaning in contemplation.

Intervening in this human intellectual process, the Christian faith confers a new dignity on matter. With the Incarnation of Christ, in the union of divinity with humanity, containing neither admixture nor confusion, something new appeared in the relationship between the divine and the human, the heavenly and the earthly. Since the Incarnation of Christ, images are not only no longer forbidden, as in the Old Testament; they actually become both legitimate and necessary. It was out of the exultation that arose in the face of the possibility of actually representing the Absolute that icons were born.

It is true that the characteristics of the icon as a profoundly theological reflection of Revelation are also to be found in the religious paintings of the West. But the icon possesses yet another dimension of meaning: it is the imprint of the celestial world on matter, and as such it becomes

*an object of veneration. Through spiritual likeness the re-
ality of holiness becomes present in the icon. So veneration of the icon of Christ is transformed into adoration of
Christ himself. By means of this link with the divine world
of God, the icon becomes an instrument of grace. This has
been the experience of Eastern Christians from the first
centuries. Contemplating these sacred images, Christians
perceive a world transfigured by the light of God, and they
receive "strength against evil, healing of body and soul,
and the consolation of the Holy Spirit," as the prayer for
the blessing of an icon expresses it.*

   *All these things need to be kept in mind while reading
this book. Then, what might begin as intellectual curios-
ity will be transformed into an authentic spiritual discovery, and the theological richness of these images will shine
as a vision that leads to opening one's heart in prayer to
the One who is the source of all truth and beauty. The icon
becomes a place of spiritual communion in rigorous
fidelity to the Revelation of Jesus Christ.*

FR. EGON SENDLER

The Image "Not Made by Human Hands"

"Thanks to the symbol, Moses knew beforehand the mystery of the tent which embraces the universe. This tent is in reality Christ, the power of God and the wisdom of God; this same wisdom of God, not made by human hands but uncreated by nature, became a creature when, because of our condition, it was necessary to produce this tent of flesh. Therefore, this tent, depending on one's point of view, is both created and uncreated. By nature it is uncreated in that it existed before time began; instead, in that it assumed a bodily form, it is created and made."

—St. Gregory of Nyssa, *De Vita Moysis*, PG 44, 382 B

The Image "Not Made by Human Hands"

> "Something...which we have seen with our own eyes,
> which we have watched
> and touched with our own hands,
> the Word of life—
> ...We are declaring to you."
>
> *(1 Jn 1:1, 3)*

According to legend, the image of the Savior "not made by human hands" reproduces the true appearance of Christ that had been impressed upon a cloth, the *mandilion*. Christ himself is supposed to have given the mandilion to King Abgar V of Edessa who, gravely ill, prayed that Christ would come to him. The significance of this legend is that it attests to the historicity of Jesus Christ, and it affirms that every representation of his likeness goes back to an initial image that was received, not fabricated; divine, not human.

Moreover, the Council of Nicaea (325) had already affirmed that testimonies regarding the features of Christ went back to Jesus himself, while the Quinisext Synod (691) established that the symbolical representations of the Incarnate Word (such as the very popular lamb) had to yield to portrayals of Christ in his humanity.

This iconographic model of the face of Christ shown against the background of a cruciform halo almost certainly originated with the display of the Shroud at Constantinople. Certainly, for Greek-speaking Christians, its name "not made by human hands" *(acheiropoietos)* possessed a special resonance related to the exclusive use of this particular phrase in the New Testament: whether it was a question of the dwelling-place of the Most High "the greater, the more perfect tent, not made by human hands" (Heb 9:11); of the new temple "not made by human hands" (Mk 14:58) that was the body of Christ; of "circumcision performed, not by human hand" (Col 2:11) because it is the gift of the Spirit of Christ; or of "a house for us from God, not made by human hands but everlasting, in the heavens" (2 Co 5:1), prepared for the faithful, one and the same adjective, *acheiropoietos,* "not made by human hands," serves to underline the sovereign majesty of God and

1. The Image "Not Made by Human Hands."

his absolute power and, at the same time, the transforming penetration of divinity into fragile and ephemeral humanity in a permanent gift of love.

This is the Christian mystery par excellence. A visual synthesis of it can be seen in the ancient Byzantine-style icon of the *Savior Not Made by Human Hands*, which was painted in the region of Novgorod at the end of the twelfth century.

A cross contained in a circle, which is itself contained in a square: a highly centralized, yet perpetually expanding pattern; in and of itself it constitutes a universal symbol of the orderly and beneficent entry of the Transcendent (the circle of the celestial vault) into the earthly reality (the square, the linear extension of the fourfold orientation of space.)

The center of the pattern of the entire icon, the source of movement, radiating outward, coincides with the ideal center of the face, situated, according to Byzantine aesthetic canons, at the root of the nose.[1] Meanwhile, the sacrificial cross of Christ (the cruciform halo) is superimposed upon the four-directional spaced earth. In this way the entire icon becomes a synthetic expression of the mystery of Creation and Redemption.

The distinct contour of the eyes and the shadows under the arches of the eyebrows augment the profundity of the gaze, while the asymmetrical arrangement of the pupils "opens out" this gaze in all directions.

Furthermore, the design of the hair, combed in waves, the symbol of time without end, indicates that Christ, the Image of the Father "not made by human hands," impressed upon created reality, is the eternal Word.

White, gold, yellow-gold and brown-ochre all form a unique and luminous chromatic blend: in Christ everything that exists has become light.

The Pantocrator

"Who is he in whom all things were created and in whom all things subsist? In whom we live, and move, and are? Who has in himself all that is from the Father? Do we not yet know, from what has been said, that he who is God over all things, as St. Paul says, is our Lord Jesus Christ? He holds in his hand everything from the Father, as he himself states: he embraces absolutely everything with his most ample grasp; he rules over everything he embraces and no one takes anything out of his hand. Therefore, if he possesses everything and governs what he possesses, who else can he be but the Pantocrator, he who rules all things?"

—St. Gregory of Nyssa, *Contra Eunomium*, PG 45, 525A

The Pantocrator

> "...the mystery of his purpose,
> ...that he would bring everything together under Christ,
>   as head,
> everything in the heavens and everything on earth."
>
> *(Ep 1:9-10)*

I n the early centuries, Christian life and sentiment were profoundly influenced by the expectation of the Lord's returning as judge at the end of time. Significantly, by the middle of the fourth century, the Church at Antioch had already introduced into the anaphora a mention of the "second coming, glorious and terrible," of the Lord. As a result of the influence of Syrian monasticism, this theme of the Parousia entered into the liturgical texts of the divine office throughout the entire Christian East.

This expectation of the second coming later broadened to include the contemplation of the only-begotten Son, the Lord of history, for whom and by whom everything was made, who recapitulated everything in himself in order to offer it back to the Father (cf. 1 Co 15:24). Maximus the Confessor expressed this vision in a beautiful synthesis: "Christ contains everything in himself as the center from which all rays emanate."[2]

This conception of Christ could not fail to be translated into some kind of figurative expression. Once the recognition of Christianity as the religion of the empire came about (fourth century), official models and forms of art were assimilated by Christian iconography. The move from the temporal sovereign to the spiritual sovereign was a normal thing: Christ in majesty, seated upon a throne in the form of a large chair, with a cushion of the cloth and purple color reserved to the emperor; or with only head and shoulders represented—but always hieratic, in the act of bestowing a blessing while holding a book in his left hand. This was the most popular image of the Lord from the fifth century on.

A substantial change in Church architecture took place in the whole Byzantine world after the Iconoclastic Period. It was a shift from the rectangular building plan to that of a Greek cross, and it was destined to lead to a further development in portrayals of Christ.[3] In fact, the new style created in the churches a place that was naturally gifted with highly meaningful symbolism: the vault of the central cupola, which coincides with the

18

2. Christ Pantocrator.

highest point, and likewise the center, of the church. Consistently reserved for the image of Christ, the cupola offered the possibility of visually conveying the message of the Word Incarnate's universal dominion over everything visible and invisible.

It should not be surprising that, in this setting, the figure of Christ was given a special title. Greek-speaking Christians had already long possessed a term which well described the nature of the dominion exercised by the Risen Lord: *Pantocrator,* "He who rules over everything."

This divine epithet used to follow the name of God the Father in the Profession of Faith: "I believe in God the Father, pantocrator—omnipotent"; and the Fathers of the Church were quick to justify its attribution to the Son also. It expressed a lively sense of the power of God always at work in creation, keeping all things in existence and, therefore, also saving them. St. Athanasius wrote: "The omnipotent and most holy Word of the Father, penetrating all things and reaching everywhere with his strength, gives light to all reality, containing and embracing everything in himself. Not a single being can remove itself from his dominion. All things receive their entire life from him and are kept in existence by him: every single creature in its individuality as well as the universe in its entirety."[4]

The idea of outstretched arms, always present in the Lord "Pantocrator," is intimately connected to the etymological meaning of the word: he who *by the strength of his arm* can rule, direct, and guide.

Probably the most powerful expression of this life-giving embrace is found in the *Pantocrator* of Monreale, an adaptation of byzantine-style iconography, located in the cupola of the rectangular basilica-structure typical of Sicilian cathedrals.

The superhuman proportions of the bust's figure, completely filling the vault of the apse, symbolically proclaim the truth of faith that the Pantocrator penetrates and fills all things with himself. The widespread embrace signifies that he enfolds everything and gives life to it all. The writing that appears on the open book: "I am the light of the world; anyone who follows me will not be walking in the dark" (Jn 8:12), along with the gesture of blessing, shows him as the Savior.[5] Finally, the inclusion of the Church triumphant—the Mother of God, the angels, the apostles and the saints—in what could be seen as the extension of the figure of Christ, further identifies the Pantocrator as the one whom the Father "made..., as he is above all things, the head of the Church; which is his Body, the fullness of him who is filled, all in all" (Ep 1:22-23).

The Savior

"*He commanded us to follow him, not because he had any need of our service, but to grant us salvation. To follow the Savior, in fact, means sharing in salvation, just as to follow the light means being surrounded by brightness.*

"*He who is in the light is surely not the one to create the light and make it shine; rather, it is the light that shines on him and illuminates him. He gives nothing to the light, but he receives from it the benefit of its splendor, as well as all its other advantages.*"

—St. Irenaeus, *Adversus Haereses,* IV, 14, 1: PG 7, 1010B

The Savior

"I am the light of the world;
anyone who follows me will not be walking in the dark
but will have the light of life."

(Jn 8:12)

The characteristics of the Pantocrator: severe and accentuated features; a reserved and impassive, sometimes even terrible expression; a powerful body, within which immense energies reside—all these aimed to illustrate a theme of great importance in the theologico-monastic environment of Constantinople: that of the Word Incarnate as the image of the Father, himself not capable of direct representation.

During the great period of Byzantine artistic creativity (ninth to the fourteenth centuries), many smaller-sized reproductions of Christ were created. Although they tended to retain the same composite structure and pattern already developed, they preferred to picture Christ as the Savior of the World, merciful and clement, the Wisdom of the Father.

In our present icon, the notation that Christ is indeed "the Savior"— *ho Sôter*—appears in Greek words under the obligatory initials of the name "Jesus Christ": IC, XP. Preserved in the Serbian monastery of Chilandari, this icon goes back to the renaissance period of the Palaeologus dynasty (fourteenth century); it is an extraordinary example of an iconographic tradition that has never been exhausted.

In the One who stands before us in this icon we see less of the omnipotent Judge. The brow and the gaze full of light suggest rather Christ as Wisdom and the Light of the world. Literally charged with a tranquil and serene strength, Christ looks into and illumines every heart; nobody is excluded from the kindness of his gaze.

This is how St. Simeon the New Theologian (tenth century) wrote about a similar image of Christ: "At the moment when everybody's gaze is fixed upon him, and when he too is gazing out at innumerable spectators, he maintains his eyes always fixed in an unchangeable position, and each viewer has the impression of being personally regarded by him, able to enjoy his conversation and be embraced by him; no one can complain about being neglected."[6]

3. Christ Pantocrator: "The Savior."

23

The time for judgement has not yet come. Even the sealed book he holds, resplendent with precious stones, with its wide red edge, which makes it appear to move towards whoever is looking at it, symbolically conveys the message of the One who will open it for us. Then there is the very delicate and unusual movement of the right hand, itself highlighted. It is as much an invitation as it is a blessing: "While you still have the light, believe in the light so that you may become children of light" (Jn 12:36).

The Master and Judge

"What was it, in fact, that reconciled God with the human race? Only this: God saw his beloved Son made man. Similarly, God is reconciled with each person individually if each person is clothed with the likeness of his only-begotten Son, is a bearer of his body and shows himself one spirit with him. Without these conditions, each individual remains 'the old man,' detestable to God and having nothing in common with him."

—Nicholas Cabasilas, *Explication de la divine liturgie,* XLIV SC 4 bis, Paris, 1967, pp. 253-255

25

The Master and Judge

"The judgements you give
are the judgements you will get,
and the standard you use
will be the standard used for you."

(Mt 7:1-2) (Text appears on the icon.)

I n Russia, as in the other countries that received Christianity from Byzantium towards the end of the first millennium, the iconographic representation of Christ Pantocrator, with only head and shoulders shown or seated upon the throne, almost always bears the name "Savior" (in Russian: *Spas), regardless of the accent placed, more or less strongly, on Christ in his function as Judge.

Generally he is shown wearing a purple tunic interwoven with gold; this is covered with a dark-blue cloak—the color of transcendence. In his left hand he holds a book either opened or closed; it is either the gospel or the book of judgement. With his right hand he bestows a blessing, holding his fingers in a position which suggests the letters of the acrostic IXΘVC: Jesus Christ, Son of God, Savior. On the cruciform halo appear the Greek letters which spell the name of Yahweh, "He Who Is" *(ho ôn)*.

The characteristics of an elongated face, with high forehead and small mouth, appear in our present icon of the Savior, which belongs to the Moscow school (fifteenth century). Even rather narrow shoulders resulting from a slight twist of the upper body contribute to the vertical movement of the entire composition. There is a noticeable difference between this and the classical proportions of the works inspired by Greek influence.

Illuminated with an interior light, the Christ figure appears to be slightly withdrawn and to look down upon the spectator. The visual axis of the icon is in fact directed downwards toward the expanse of the open gospel, which is thereby doubly accentuated. Whether the book is open or closed in these icons, it always has a profoundly symbolic value: as opposed to a sealed scroll, it signifies the Revelation of God that accompanied Christ's coming.

"I saw that in the right hand of the One sitting on the throne there was *a scroll....* But there was no one, in heaven or on the earth or under the

4. Christ Pantocrator: "The Savior."

earth, who was able to open the scroll and read it.... Then I saw...a Lamb that seemed to have been sacrificed;.... The Lamb came forward to take the scroll from the right hand of the One sitting on the throne..." (Rv 5:1-7 passim). Only the Lamb of God, the Incarnate Word himself, could effect "the passage from the book as a rolled-up scroll to the book displayed in squared and extended form."[7] Only Christ, that is, could reveal the meaning of history which manifests the saving will of the Father. The book thus becomes the book of life.

The Lord's hand, in its delicate gesture, is at the cross section of the two internal movements of the icon, and it creates the balance between the expression of his sovereignty as divine Judge and his gaze, which penetrates the recesses of the heart.

The Image of the Father

"*The Lord took on a human nature and came to us. He nevertheless remained hidden after this manifestation, or, yet more typically divine, in this manifestation itself, so that what was expressed remained mysterious and what was grasped remained unknown.*"

—Dionysius the Areopagite, *Ep. III*; PG 3, 1079 B

The Image of the Father

> "Everything has been entrusted to me by my Father;
> and no one knows who the Son is except the Father,
> and who the Father is except the Son
> and those to whom the Son chooses to reveal him."
>
> *(Lk 10:22)*

T he painting of icons was a service officially recognized by the Church, inasmuch as it presented theology—words about God—through images. Thus, for centuries the painting of icons was entrusted only to men totally consecrated to God. This consecration of theirs was seen as a help in imprinting upon the bright mirror of their souls "the pure image of spotless beauty."[8]

The goal of the most common spiritual Way of Eastern monasticism, called *hesychasm* (from the Greek *hesychia*=quiet), consisted precisely in this: everything hinged upon "recalling Jesus": through constant prayer, through the sacramental life, and through the purification of the senses—especially through the renunciation of every activity of the imagination. The result of this, as Gregory Palamas suggested, was to become radiant like the angels with the same original Light, so as to manifest in oneself the fascination of God's hidden beauty and his brilliant and inaccessible splendor.

This idea of the transparency of God shining through the spiritual person is intimately connected with the "presence" believed to be contained in the icon which justifies its veneration: the spiritual presence of the holy Person, or of the Mystery being represented, made possible by the creative spiritual journey of the icon painter himself.

We encounter the radiant presence of the mystery of Christ in the icon of the *Savior* by Andrei Rublev (1360—c. 1430), the greatest of the Russian iconographers. Here the capacity of a person of the Spirit to reflect uncreated Beauty and Goodness becomes almost tangible. And, by returning to the source, we understand that the foundation of this mediation through the senses is Christ himself.

In fact, in Christ, according to the thought of the great St. Irenaeus, the manifestation of the mystery of the Father—"the Son is the visible image of the Father"[9]—is joined to the restoration of the created image which

30

5. The Savior (Deёsis of Zvenigorod).

is man: "In times past it was said that man was made in the image of God, but it did not appear as such because the Word, the image in accordance with which man had been made, still remained invisible. For that reason it was easy to lose sight of the resemblance. But when the Word of God became flesh, he confirmed the divine-human resemblance. He displayed the true image, himself becoming that which was his image, and he firmly reestablished that resemblance, rendering man similar to the invisible Father through the Word who was visible."[10]

All observers agree in stressing the intense humanity depicted in this icon of the Savior. It is the central figure in the *Deësis of Zvenigorod*.[11] The typical hieratic rigidity of the Pantocrator has disappeared from this work. Lifelike movement is suggested by the slight torsion of the three-quarter representation of the upper body and by a certain asymmetry of the face, even though the face is depicted frontally. He seems to have just turned, at that very moment, to gaze at the person standing before him.

Extreme delicacy is the dominant note of this icon: the roseate color, the blond beard through which the contours of the face can just barely be distinguished, the small mouth, the subtle line of the arch of the eyebrows, the clear hazel eyes. All of these features contribute to an impression of youth, sweetness and goodness.

Yet the icon depicts Christ the Lord. One who looks on him with freedom of spirit cannot but perceive how the human qualities depicted in this image actually possess an absolute value. Christ is not merely an ideal figure of human goodness; he is Goodness itself, Meekness and Mercy, and he is also Truth and Justice, in that perfect unity of Justice and Goodness, which is humanly impossible, but proper to God.

Several elements of this icon's composition doubtless contribute to these double values: the unnaturally elongated proportions of the entire figure, along with the pronounced vertical tendency of all the lines; the tremendous strength expressed in the neck which, to some degree, contrasts with the sweetness of the face; the light which plays upon the upper cheeks under the eyes and upon the forehead and which exalts the whole upper part of the face. But how the holy monk, Andrei Rublev, succeeded in revealing in this icon the mystery of God made man remains a secret of artistic creativity combined with personal faith.

The Savior amid the Heavenly Powers

"We declare that Christ will come again. There is not only one coming; there will be a Second Coming, more glorious than the first. The first coming, in fact, bore the seal of suffering; the next will bear a crown of divine royalty....

"In his first coming Christ was wrapped in swaddling clothes and laid in a manger; in the second he will be wrapped in light as with a mantle. The first time he accepted the cross without refusing its dishonor; the next time he will come forth full of glory and accompanied by bands of angels....

"He shall come therefore: our Lord Jesus Christ shall come from heaven; he will come in glory at the end of the created world, on the last day. This will mark the end of this world, and the birth of a new world."

—St. Cyril of Jerusalem, *Cat. XV;* PG 33, 870A; 871C

The Savior amid the Heavenly Powers

"Beyond the solid surface above their heads,
there was what seemed like a sapphire,
in the form of a throne.
High above on the form of a throne
was a form with the appearance of a human being."

(Ezk 1:26)

With its immense, contained strength, sharp detail and formidable energy expanding around a nucleus of light—who could imagine that this marvelous icon of Andrei Rublev's measures less than twenty centimeters in height? This leads us to ask whether the artist did not specifically will to express through the paradox of such littleness the immeasurable glory of the One who sits upon the cherubim.

This icon possesses a vision of greatly concentrated power, in which many aspects of the mystery of the Incarnate Word converge. Seated on a throne supported by the wheels of cherubim, surrounded by seraphim, Christ appears, above all, as the Creator and Lord of the whole universe, which orders itself around him in accordance with the combined visions of Ezekiel and Isaiah: see the square rhombus of the earth, in red, and the oval-shaped heavens in dark green. The throne, carefully delineated in white, expresses a cosmic symbolism, with its cubed seat surmounted by a circular arch; the rectangular footrest on which the Lord places his feet further emphasizes his Lordship: "...with heaven my throne and earth my footstool" (Is 66:1).

The brilliant red of the two square rhombi, set off by the dark green that separates them, evokes the mystery of the One who at the same time is both impenetrable Light and impenetrable Obscurity: "That obscurity," in the words of Dionysius the Areopagite, "to which justice has still not been done when it is said that it yet shines as the brightest of all lights amidst the blackest of all darknesses." But the figure, with a "brilliance like amber" (Ezk 1:27)—of Christ the Word, which emerges so distinctly from the fiery red background and successfully tones down its brightness, announces by the silent evidence of the vision that the divine darkness, shining as the brightest of all lights, has manifested itself as Light for all humanity.

6. The Savior amid the Heavenly Powers.

This central theme of Eastern monasticism—the manifestation in the Incarnate Word of "uncreated Light,"—cannot have been far from the mind of the blessed monk Andrei. His life spanned the end of the fourteenth and the beginning of the fifteenth centuries and coincided with the greatest expansion in Russian history of hesychast spirituality.

Recalling the "chariot of Yahweh," the winged wheels of fire connect the symbolism of the throne with the outer four-part form containing the Tetramorph, the "four living creatures" of Ezekiel's vision—man, lion, ox and eagle: "I looked; a stormy wind blew from the north, a great cloud with flashing fire...and in the middle what seemed to be four living creatures.... they did not turn as they moved; each one moved straight forward" (Ezk 1:4-5, 9). This was already considered a symbol of the provident omnipresence of God; but in the new era of grace these four elements came to signify the Good News of salvation proclaimed by the evangelists to the four corners of the earth.

Christ the Lord holds the book of the Gospel, rendered in pure white, the most luminous spot in the whole icon. Four bundles of golden rays issue from him, the Center from which the new creation pours forth.

Even with all of this, however, the richness of the various aspects of the mystery of Christ as depicted in this icon is not yet exhausted. Clothed as he is in a golden-threaded robe, Christ appears like a flash of lightning against the icon's double background. He is the Judge of the Eighth Day. He is the Lord of History. He is the One of whom Scripture says: "For he is to be king until he has made his enemies his footstool" (1 Co 15:25).

However, if we consider the serious, searching expression of his face, interiorly illuminated as it is, in the light of the words written on the open book—"Come to me, all you who labour and are overburdened, and I will give you rest" (Mt 11:28)—we discover that he is also the Merciful One, the Friend of humankind, he who hands down a law of liberty and who judges according to this law.

The Virgin of the Sign

"Thus, this Son of God, our Lord, who is the Word of the Father, is also the Son of man, because from Mary, who was generated by human beings and was herself a human being, he had a human birth and became Son of man.

"Therefore, the Lord himself gave us a sign, in both the heights and the depths, a sign that man had not asked for, since no one would ever have imagined that a virgin could conceive and bear a son while continuing to be a virgin, and that the fruit of this childbirth would be 'God-with-us'; that he would descend into the depths of the earth to search for the lost sheep (which was, in effect, his own creature); and then that he would ascend into heaven to offer and present to the Father this humanity, which, by this means had been found again."

—St. Irenaeus of Lyons, *Adversus Haereses, II*, 19, 3; PG 7, 941A

The Virgin of the Sign

> "The Lord will give you a sign in any case:
> It is this: the young woman is with child
> and will give birth to a son
> whom she will call Immanuel."
>
> *(Is 7:14)*

T he first image of Christ "not made by human hands" was recognized as having had a historical origin. Analogously, ecclesiastical tradition attributed the first images of the Virgin Mary to St. Luke the Evangelist. This expressed a double truth: that the person of Mary was linked historically to the events of the Redemption, and that the role of Mary could only be really understood in the light of faith.

As was the case with the first representations of the Lord, so those of the Virgin Mother came out of an already existing patrimony of iconography, to which belonged the image of the *pietas*—a praying figure with hands raised towards heaven. This figure symbolized reverence towards God and became in Christian art the iconographic sign for representing the deceased Christian and, in particular, the martyr—model of the true believer, who hopes for and expects life in Christ.

This figure, however, with its arms raised symmetrically upwards, unfolded its symbolic richness when by the fifth century it was applied to the Virgin Mary: the gesture of the hand with its palm turned upwards expressed the expectation of the gift to be received from God; and, at the same time, it expressed a total readiness to be "filled by the Most High." These raised hands renounce any autonomous intervention in history; they create an invisible receptacle which God can fill and from which flows, as from the basin of a fountain, the true water of life.[12]

It is not surprising, therefore, that this image of the Virgin praying— called *Blachernitissa*, from the name of the sanctuary in Constantinople where a similar image received particular veneration—was completed in the ninth century by the addition of the Child depicted inside a medallion. This idea was inspired by the customs of the imperial court: just as the images of the emperor and of the consuls were presented to their subjects in order

7. The Praying Virgin, "Great Panagia," or "Virgin of the Sign of Yaroslavl."

39

to be honored, so the empresses and other court dignitaries carried on their chests embroidered images of the sovereign as "signs" of his supreme authority.[13]

The Praying Virgin with the Child in a medallion is thus not a historical representation of the Mother with Child. Rather she is, precisely, the Virgin of the Sign, the Russian name for this kind of icon. She is the one who, according to the prophecy of Isaiah, presents to the world the advent of the era of salvation through the Incarnation of the Word.

As the privileged carrier, indeed, the protagonist of this "sign," the praying Virgin is at the same time necessarily the one who intercedes for humanity and transmits divine grace: "In order to defend our cause, she extends her immaculate hands over the whole world."[14]

From the apse of the cathedral of Yaroslavl, the majestic Byzantine icon of the *Great Panagia*, "the All Holy," radiated down upon all who contemplated it, a veritable proclamation of the gift of the Father: "The Word of God, Jesus Christ, our Lord, in his superabundant love, was made what we are, in order that we might be made what he is."[15]

This icon was commissioned for the new stone cathedral of the royal palace, dedicated in 1215 by Constantine the Wise, Prince of Rostov and Vladimir, a great connoisseur and lover of art and of the Greco-Byzantine culture to the point that he was styled "a second Solomon."[16]

Larger than life-size, this figure of the praying Virgin, with its classic proportions, was integrated into a perfectly balanced context. It is not difficult to observe how the flaring of her mantle serves to join the inverted triangle of the upper part of the icon with the large rectangle of the lower part. The first is clearly traced by the upraised arms of Mary and by the circles geometrically placed at the angles, while the second is outlined by the large rug which serves as a pedestal.

The purple of the *homophorion,* or combination veil and mantle, like the red of the rug with its rich foliage design, is in perfect harmony with the dark green of the dress. The warm gold of the background shines through even the folds of the garments, where usually the color is given a brighter overtone. The end result is an effect of brilliant light rendered even more intense by the white haloes.

The delicate features of the faces are a continuous source of new discoveries.

The Virgin Hodigitria

"God, wishing to create the image of all beauty and reveal his resemblance to angels as well as to men, fashioned Mary with his own total beauty, uniting in her all the particular beauties distributed to creatures according to their nature and constituting her as the summary ornament of all creatures, visible and invisible; or, better, presenting her as a synthesis of all the divine, angelic, and human beauties, indeed, as the supreme beauty, gracing both worlds."

—Gregory Palamas, *In Dormitionem;* PG 151, 468 AB

The Virgin Hodigitria

"You are wholly beautiful, my beloved,
and without a blemish."

(Sg 4:7)

With the triumph of Christianity in the fourth century and the proclamation at the Council of Ephesus (431) of Mary as *Theotókos,* the Mother of God, the way was opened up for picturing the Mother and Child as inspired by imperial iconography. There multiplied in the East as well as in the West images called "Majesty," of the Virgin seated upon a throne in the act of presenting the Child-Son of God.

This iconographic model gave rise in the Byzantine world to two kinds of representations of Mary which were both equally regal and hieratic: the *Panagia Nikopeia,* where she is standing or seated, severe and majestic, holding the Child before her with both hands; and the *Panagia Hodigitria,* where she is depicted standing, seated, or with the upper body alone shown holding the Child in one arm. Following the victory over iconoclasm (843), both these types of icons were widely diffused, along with the *Blachernitissa.* This was partly because of the constant recourse to the Mother of God in both public and private devotion, and partly because of the birth of a great number of artistic workshops that produced copies of the icons venerated in the great sanctuaries of Constantinople.

The *Virgin Hodigitria,* of which this icon of Byzantine origin (fourteenth century) is a very beautiful example, took its distinctive name from a church in Constantinople (Hodigôn "of the guides"), where an image of this type was venerated as the work of St. Luke the Evangelist himself. Later, this reference to the "guides" acquired a personal significance, becoming "She who points the way."

The Christ Child, given the features of an adult, is seated upright on his Mother's arm. As the Savior, he is blessing; meanwhile he holds the scroll of the gospels; his gold-woven garment, based on the model of the ancient sages, is the royal and priestly dress of the Incarnate Word.

The Mother, robed in a mantle of dark purple bordered with gold, is not exercising, as is usually the case in Western art, a protective role

8. The Virgin Hodigitria.

43

towards her Son. Rather, she is presenting him to mankind, interceding with him at the same time. Her right hand, in a gesture of great richness, appears to receive and to offer simultaneously. Her facial expression is serious, full of regal serenity; her gaze is directly aimed at the spectator.

A kind of spiritual architecture presides over the composition of the faces. The rather unrealistic magnification of the dome of the head, seat of the spirit which exercises dominion over the instincts of the body, points to the divine resemblance that the human creature possesses. The facial lineaments themselves, if geometrically reconstructed, suggest a living temple in which the delicate column of the nasal bridge supports the arches of the eyebrows, beneath which the eyes open wide for contemplation and from which an interior light bursts forth.[17]

Even the composition of colors has a spiritual significance. The vast, dark surface of the Virgin's mantle stands out as a particular mass against the gold background; this is the ideal chromatic environment of Byzantine icons and mosaics. Not subordinate to any source of light, the gold is not even a "color" in the proper sense of the word. Rather, it is an absolute value of luminosity which does not admit of that dualism of light and shadow without which nothing on earth is even imaginable.[18]

Through such symbolic visual equations did Byzantine art attempt to express the truth of the Christian faith that human persons and events belonging to the history of salvation are "immersed" in the divine milieu.

Under the obligatory initials MP ΘV, "Mother of God," pointing to the dignity of Mary, the icon painter added the honorific title *"hè perìbleptos"*: "She who is marvelous."[19] Grace and beauty are joined together in the Purest One, manifested by God as the "synthesis of all the divine, angelic, and human beauties, indeed the supreme beauty gracing both worlds."[20]

The Virgin Hodigitria in the West

"*We salute you, O Mary, Mother of God, venerable treasure of all that has been created!*

"*Rejoice, you who received in your virginal womb him who is infinite and immense.*

"*Through you the Holy Trinity is adored and glorified. Through you the precious cross is celebrated in every corner of the earth.*

"*Through you believers arrive at the grace of holy baptism. Through you flows the oil of gladness.*

"*Through you churches have been founded throughout the world. Through you therefore everything becomes joy.*"

—St. Cyril of Alexandria, *Hom. 4;* PG 77, 991 BC

The Virgin Hodigitria in the West

"Do whatever he tells you."
(Jn 2:5)

T he icon of the *Virgin Hodigitria* preserved in the abbey church of St. Nilus at Grottaferrata (Rome) is both similar to and very different from the *Virgin Hodigitria* of the classical Byzantine type. The example reproduced here allows us to cast a glance on the complex world of cultural ties between the Byzantine East and the countries of the Latin world, in particular, Italy, at the dawn of the second Christian millennium.

Even the beginnings of this particular abbey are significant. It was founded in the eleventh century by St. Nilus, a much venerated monk of Greek ancestry who came from Rossano in Calabria. Like many other monks of his day in Calabria and in the lands around Otranto, he had to leave this area because of the continual invasions of the Saracens. Various monastic communities of the Greek rite, therefore, took refuge in central Italy, while maintaining their ties with their sister communities in the South.

Within this historical context, a century later, the Crusades were undertaken. The presence in Grottaferrata of this particular icon of the *Virgin Hodigitria* is easier to understand.

Painted in all probability in Cyprus around the beginning of the thirteenth century,[21] it made its way to Latium through Apulia which, at that time, was a real nerve center for travel to the Holy Land and the Greek islands.

It is of little importance whether this work was executed by a Cypriot artist, or by one of the numerous French and Italian artists who came to Cyprus and Palestine with the Crusaders and founded flourishing artistic workshops there, adopting the Greek style. What is to be noted is that, in thirteenth-century Florence, this "Greek style" constituted the new style of painting.

The Virgin of Grottaferrata bears witness to a transformation of the classic Byzantine model—hieratic and spiritualized—towards a more naturalistic type of icon.

9. The Virgin Hodigitria.

The reasons for this change in style—not seen in Russian iconography, which is a direct offshoot of Byzantium—are various. They include: a greater liberty in the Byzantine province concerning models of the official art of the Empire; the influence of the more narrative and ornamental Syrian art; and, in a still too meagerly recognized measure—the contribution made by Western artists.

However that may be, the difference lies not so much in the greater importance accorded to the sphere of sentiment—in fact, the same can be seen in the classical Byzantine *Eleoúsa,* "the Merciful One"—as it does in the lessening of the intense interior life which characterizes the iconography of pure Byzantine inspiration.

In the case of this particular icon, some of the elements illustrate the change we have been discussing: for instance, the relief achieved by the volumes of the faces through the strong contrast between the basic greenish flesh tones of some areas and those larger surfaces given an apricot tint; the natural proportions of the Child's head; the strong line of the Virgin's nose, a typical facial trait of middle-eastern women; and the ornately decorated border, clearly of Syrian inspiration. Also, and no less important, is the disappearance of the fine white illuminations indicating interior light.

It is clear that a new and different sensibility is manifesting itself in this icon. But it would be a mistake to deny its value *a priori*, although we know that it was to lead to an art that would be characterized by purely human expression—too human—of religious themes rather than by the profound tension contained in the Byzantine attempt to portray the Invisible.[22]

The Virgin of Tenderness of Vladimir

"The vine of the Spouse, planted in the fertile land of God (that is, in the depth of the soul), and watered by divine truths, grows to maturity, producing a cluster of grapes in which the true gardener and vine-dresser may be recognized.

"O blessed plot whose fruit bears resemblance to the beauty of the divine Spouse! In fact, because Christ is the true light, true life and true holiness, as the Book of Wisdom says, as well as all other riches, if someone becomes like the Spouse through the fruit that one bears, when looking at the cluster of one's conscience, he sees the Spouse himself, because that person's shining and spotless life reflects the light of truth."

—St. Gregory of Nyssa, *In Cantica*, Hom. IV; PG 44, 829 AB

The Virgin of Tenderness of Vladimir

"His mother stored up all these things in her heart."

(Lk 2:51)

T owards the end of the first millennium, in harmony with the greater emphasis being placed on the total mystery of Christ—his Incarnation and salvific death—which followed the movement known as iconoclasm, the figure of the *Theotókos* began to be humanized. This is especially seen in the type of icon known as the *Eleoúsa,* "the Merciful One," which presents the Virgin inclined in prayer, either alone or with the Child resting on her arm with his cheek against hers.

This attitude was intended to express not so much the maternal tenderness of Mary as her power to elicit tenderness in her Son; she is always the one who intercedes with her Son for the sake of the human race, she is the Merciful One. The Russian term applied to this type of icon, *Umilenie,* also bears the same meaning of compassionate tenderness.

The Byzantine icon of the Virgin *Eleoúsa* shown here was brought to Russia at the beginning of the twelfth century where it remained for a long period in the city of Vladimir, after which it has been named. This icon proclaims through the ages the marvels of her who is a mother while remaining a virgin. Perhaps her gaze, which does not rest on the Child but is at once farsighted and turned to an interior vision, is the best expression of this mystery of Mary.

She really and truly bore the divine Son, according to the flesh, but she consented to God's making her fruitful because she was totally unified in her own being and free from outside influence, a pure, loving creature: "The Holy Spirit will come upon you" (Lk 1:35).

A great spiritual writer expressed it thus: "When one receives God into one's being, that is good, and in this receptivity one is a virgin. But if God can render a soul productive, it is better, because to bear fruit through a gift received is to show gratitude for that gift."[23]

50

10. The Virgin of Tenderness of Vladimir.

Gratitude excludes any sentiment of personal possession. As a Virgin Mother, Mary does not "possess" her own Son, but unceasingly consents to his being born from her and welcomes him as an absolute gift.

This radical detachment from her own Son is the primary spiritual reality in the life of the Virgin Mother.

Conscious of her being a virgin in this sense, the Son could ask her from his cross for the supreme renunciation. "Woman, this is your son" (Jn 19:27). By this Christ allowed her to participate in a unique way in the mystery of redemption as the Mother of all humanity. In this perspective, her distant gaze signifies the attention she gives to her children who invoke her, to sinners who ask for the intercession of "the Merciful One."

The Belozersk Virgin of Tenderness

"That which the participated being is by nature, necessarily transforms the being that is participating. So, since virtue is the fragrance of Christ, and since the disposition to love really effects union with the beloved, that which we love we ourselves become: *namely, the fragrance of Christ. One who loves the Beautiful becomes beautiful; goodness transforms the one who has received it."*

—St. Gregory of Nyssa, *In Ecclesiasten;* PG 44, 738D-739A

53

The Belozersk Virgin of Tenderness

> "When the completion of the time came,
> God sent his Son, born of a woman...."
>
> *(Ga 4:4)*

T his icon of the Mother of God of Belozersk, painted in the thirteenth century near Novgorod, brings into consideration the mystery of the Mother and Child against the background of its historical dimension. The style of the icon lends itself well both to a deep faith and to the realistic outlook on life characteristic of this ancient and flourishing citizens' republic, which served as an open window between East and West by means of its peaceful commercial exchanges.

In the upper corners of the icon the Archangels Michael and Gabriel, clothed in white garments suffused with divine light, testify to God's fidelity to his promise: Michael, in his traditional role as guardian of paradise following humanity's fall and witness to the first promise of salvation (cf. Gn 3:15); and Gabriel, the messenger of the realization of God's plan in the fullness of time.

Eighteen medallions appear on the outer frame of the icon. They represent the prophets of the Old Testament who foretold the Messiah and the saints and martyrs who witnessed his salvific coming.

The gold which is woven into the garment of the Incarnate Word and which frames the face of the Virgin Mother brightens the dark brown of the mantle, while the clear diagonal line of the Child's bare legs provides a marked contrast with the emergent dynamism of the halos, whose pure red sets them off conspicuously against the cold, clear, silver background.

Diffusing itself, the great reserve of warm light found in the central portion of the icon falls rhythmically on the halos within the medallions, but above all it rests and tones itself down in the intense blue of the frame.

The colors here make no attempt to imitate nature. Rather, they are employed in pure form, regulated by the order of the composition and the symbolic message it intends to transmit: it is the concept that inspires the color scheme.

11. The Belozersk Virgin of Tenderness.

The Igorevsk Virgin of Tenderness

"The Church already participates in a real way in the inheritance of the kingdom through the innumerable choirs of souls she has sent to heaven to settle there, whom blessed Paul calls: 'the whole Church of first-born…, enrolled as citizens of heaven' (Heb 12:23). But she has not yet obtained the kingdom for those of her children who are on the way towards 'the prize of God's heavenly call' (Phil 3:14), that is, those who are still in this life and whose end is uncertain, and also for those who have already passed on without the hope that everything will be favorable and secure. That is why the Church commemorates the death of the Lord. The Church also commemorates the saints who have achieved perfection and those souls who have not; it gives thanks for the former and offers supplication for the latter.

"We give thanks, declares the Church, because with your death you opened the doors of life, because you chose a Mother from among us, because a human being was raised into such glory, because we have ambassadors to you from our own race, because you have given to members of our own family the liberty of approaching you."

—Nicholas Cabasilas, *Explication de la divine Liturgie*, IX-X, XII, SC 4 bis, Paris, 1957, p. 97

The Igorevsk Virgin of Tenderness

> "With one heart all these joined
> constantly in prayer,
> together with...Mary the mother of Jesus."
>
> *(Ac 1:14)*

his icon of the Virgin was painted at Vologda in northern Russia. Later the wide band around it was added, with its variety of figures of Novgorodian inspiration. It is a beautiful example of artistic composition based on polychromy.

The fundamental colors—yellow, red and blue—are placed side by side without any intermediate tones or shadings in an abstract relationship tied to their dynamic values of resplendence or depth. This signifies that the colors are nothing else but types of light, and that the icon itself is a manifestation of God's light reflected in his divinized creatures, those who have already regained full resemblance to the divine Image.

As Dionysius the Areopagite wrote: "In its simplicity, in its goodness, in its fundamental perfection, the beauty proper to God communicates to each being, according to the latter's merit, a part of its own light and perfects it by re-clothing it with its particular form."[24]

Surrounded by figures of prophets, martyrs and confessors, this icon of the Mother of God—the Most Pure One in whom the divine image shines forth in its fullness—serves as a joyous testimony to the reality of the kingdom of the elect with the Father in his Son Jesus Christ.

Christ remains the true center of the icon (as is normally the case with the iconostases of the Russian Church). The mystery of Christ's saving Incarnation, represented in its historical realization by the Child with the Mother, finds itself transposed into the sphere of eternity in the upper border of the icon: the countenance of Christ adored by the cherubim and seraphim is also the countenance of the Lamb who was slain, "since he lives forever to intercede for [us]" (Heb 7:25).

The prayers of the whole Church unceasingly converge towards Christ, and these prayers, in turn, rise incessantly from Christ to the Father.

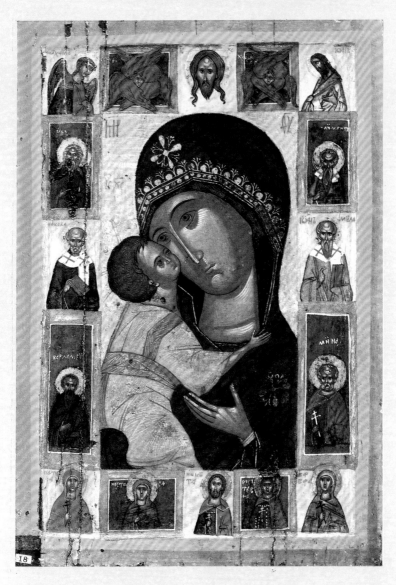

12. The Igorevsk Virgin of Tenderness.

59

The Yaroslavl Virgin of Tenderness

"According to the reliable testimony of the Word, the Bride is a well-spring of living water whose current descends from Lebanon. Who could ever fully express the marvels set forth by this comparison? It would seem impossible to elevate her any further, since she resembles every aspect of Beauty's archetypal form.

"Her own wellspring mirrors perfectly the Source; her own life—the Life; her water—the Water of Life. God's Word is alive; the soul that receives this Word is equally alive. This water flows from God, as the Source of all declares: 'I have my origin in God and have come from him' (Jn 8:42). And it is the Source that contains what flows into the well of the soul, which becomes a reservoir of the living water whose streams flow down from Lebanon."

—St. Gregory of Nyssa, *In Cantica, Hom.* IX; PG 44, 977 BD.

The Yaroslavl Virgin of Tenderness

"I was leading them with human ties,
with leading-strings of love,...
I was like someone lifting an infant
to his cheek, ...I bent down to feed him."
(Ho 11:4)

This Virgin of Yaroslavl, with its superb elegance and grace, illustrates the degree of refinement achieved by the fifteenth century school of Moscow; the icon also manifests a degree of pathos unknown to the more classical Byzantine icons. Here the theme of tenderness relates not principally to the intercessory power of the Mother but rather becomes the primary content of the relationship between the two persons, Mother and Child.

Even though the Virgin Mother continues to gaze into the distance, there are many other features of the icon which express the intensity of the emotions involved: the greater inclination of the head; the long neck which accompanies the movement of the face, increasing the impression of delicacy, indeed almost of frailty; the left hand lightly touching the head of the Child with the mere suggestion of an embrace; the tapering right hand alive and vibrant in prayer, nicely closing the spacious oval formed by the hands and faces.

The Child, as usual, is portrayed as an adult, with his head, unrealistically but very significantly, shaped in the circle of perfection. He himself perfectly harmonizes with his Mother: snuggled up against her, partly covered by her mantle, the Child grasps the garment's edge with one hand while the other hand rests firmly and securely against her cheek. The white garment of the King of Glory reflects upon the two faces like a fountain of light, making them stand out from the rest of the image.

As in all the icons of the *Eleoúsa* type, the Child is looking at the Mother. He acknowledges in her the fullness of her gift of self. Because of her total openness to God, she appears eminently vulnerable, and this vulnerability, in turn, arouses a sentiment of tenderness in the Child-God: the unimaginable tenderness of the Creator for his creature, corresponding to the creature's wondering tenderness towards the Creator who, in assuming a human nature, entrusted himself to her, becoming radically vulnerable himself.

62

13. The Yaroslavl Virgin of Tenderness.

The Order of the Deësis

"The pillars indicate the difference between the sensible and intellectual worlds, and they act as a kind of firmament dividing spiritual realities from material ones. They also indicate with respect to the altar which is Christ, how those who preach Christ and confirm our faith in him are themselves pillars of the Church. And thus the archway which ties the pillars together signifies the link of love and communion in Christ between the saints on earth and those in heaven.

"For the same reason, above the archway, in the center, among the holy icons, we find the Savior himself, and, next to him, on either side, his Mother and St. John the Baptist, as well as angels and archangels, apostles and other saints—all presented so we might understand that just as Christ abides in heaven with his saints, so he also abides here with us and he will come again."

—Simon of Thessalonica, *De Sacro Templo;* PG 155, 345 CD

The Order of the Deësis

"You are fellow-citizens with the holy
people of God and part of God's household.
You are built upon the foundations
of the apostles and prophets,
and Christ Jesus himself is the cornerstone."

(Ep 2:19-20)

T he image of Christ seated on his throne with his Mother on his right and St. John the Baptist on his left, both in an attitude of supplication, constitutes the composition entitled "the Deësis," or "Prayer." This triad is a distinctly seventh-century Byzantine creation. It presupposes, on the one hand, an enhanced sensitivity among Christians to the theme of Christ's second coming, and, on the other hand, the practice of praying through the intercession of the saints. The Deësis was destined to become an integral part of internal church architecture.

Where would it be located? Actually, a place had already been developed for it from the third century on. There is evidence from that period of the existence of a separation between the sanctuary and the nave of the church. Consisting of a wooden grille or of pillars surmounted by an archway, this dividing structure became known as an iconostasis. It disappeared in the West near the beginning of the Middle Ages, but it remained as a characteristic element of Byzantine-Greek rite churches. Soon it began to be adorned with figures of the Mother of God and of angels and saints, all grouped around the central figure of the Savior or the cross.

It is not surprising that after the victory over iconoclasm (in 843) the painting of icons on this structure became a common practice. The iconostasis was intended to symbolize the unbridgeable gap between the human and the divine, and to show at the same time that the gap had in fact been bridged, thanks to the intercession of Christ, the eternal Mediator, and of the Church already in glory.

By the thirteenth century there existed in Russia iconostases consisting of many icons arranged side by side. Only by the fifteenth century did they assume a definite order around the nucleus of the Deësis; this order became typical in Byzantine-Slavic rite churches. Representing in terms of salvation history both the present time of the Church and the eschatology of Christ's second coming (the Parousia), the basic triad of the Deësis was amplified and completed by the addition of other eminent examples of holiness, both earthly and heavenly: apostles, bishops, theologians, martyrs, ascetics and angels.

Placed immediately above the entrance to the sanctuary, the Deësis is so arranged as to express the mystery of the Church united to Christ. The faithful who approach this "royal door" (as the central door to the sanctuary was called), to receive Communion can "see" that by doing so they are joined in communion with the saints celebrating the heavenly liturgy in the presence of the Lord himself and interceding for all the living.

This presence of the Church Triumphant became all the more real once Theophanes the Greek had decorated the iconostasis in the cathedral of the Annunciation in Moscow's Kremlin (1405) with figures that were life-size to compensate for their distance from the faithful. This feature became common in subsequent iconostases, notably influencing their composition through sober essential lines, and by a harmonious ensemble of colors.

The order of the Deësis from the school of Novgorod (fifteenth century) here reproduced allows us to experience what a degree of harmonious unity the iconographers could achieve, while succeeding to transmit the calm and solemn rhythm of the celestial liturgy.

Proceeding upwards in a dramatization of salvation history in reverse, the orderly series of the Deësis is crowned with another series of icons picturing the major Church feasts, and therefore, the major events in the life of Christ. Still higher is yet another series—which could be divided in two—depicting the expectations of the Old Testament, represented by prophets bearing scrolls containing the prophecies of the Incarnation, and by the patriarchs to whom God had promised his covenant even before the people of Israel.

The center of everything is Christ: he is the Awaited One, he is the One who came and who is sacramentally present in the Church; he is the One who will come again to restore everything to the Father. In him we "have no fear in approaching the throne of grace" (Heb 4:16), so that the designs hidden in God before the ages might be made manifest.

14. The Order of the Deësis.

From a Deësis—The Mother of God

"The foundation of the Church is the creation of a new universe. According to the prophecy of Isaiah, a new heaven was created in the Church, which was, in St. Paul's words, firmness of faith in Christ. A new earth was shaped, open to the rain which fell upon it. A new human was formed, renewed from above in the image of the Creator. And a new species of celestial bodies appeared, about which was said: 'You are the light of the world....'

"And thus, just as one who looks at the sensible world and learns the wisdom which is manifested in its beauty ascends through these visible things to invisible beauty, so whoever contemplates this new Cosmos in the Church, sees in the Church the One who is 'all in all.'"

—St. Gregory of Nyssa, *In Cantica, Hom.* XIII; PG 44, 1049B-D; 1051A

From a Deësis—The Mother of God

> "The consort at your right hand
>   in gold of Ophir."
>
> *(Ps 45:9)*

The Mother of God in the Deësis of Theophanes the Greek (1340-1410) is one of the few great works of Russian religious art which is still in its original place: on the iconostasis in the Cathedral of the Annunciation in Moscow's Kremlin.

In contrast with the figure of the Savior resplendent in white and gold and set within a fiery red rhombus, the Mother is uniquely presented in a solid midnight blue unit. From the apex of an extremely simple structure (a slanted isosceles triangle) the warm colors of the face radiate: the brown and yellow ochres of the flesh, with a clear red lightly touching the cheeks and eyelids, following the line of the nose, and ending at the silent and serious mouth.

White light literally gushes out in parallel streams from the corners of the eye nearest the beholder; this makes her gaze resplendent, accentuates the fineness of the nose and highlights the chin. Then, as if crystallized in the watery blue of the edge of the bonnet, it crowns the face and reflects from the deep blue of the mantle.

Fashioned only out of depth and light, the Virgin leans slightly forward, raising her hands in supplication.

Beautiful, yes, but with a kind of hidden beauty. Beautiful according to a style that calls into play a certain type of aesthetic perception. Looking at her there spontaneously comes to mind the expression: spiritual beauty. And so it is.

The great Greek painter Theophanes, like all true artists, was a man of his time, "an illustrious sage and an eminently gifted philosopher."[25] The only works of his that have come down to us are those painted in Russia. He expressed with an unequaled intensity the aesthetic concept of hesychasm, the current of spirituality which spread through Eastern Christianity in the fourteenth century and which exerted a lasting and determining influence on Russian iconography.

15. The Virgin (Deësis).

Since "only the mind is capable of contemplating true beauty,"[26] that is, the absolute beauty of God; and since, on the other hand, the Christian life cannot prescind from the mediation of sense images established once for all in the mystery of the Incarnation, both the creation and the appreciation of beauty presuppose a person's true spiritual renewal and the acquisition of new senses: "The renewing Spirit provides new eyes and new ears. No longer as a person does one regard with the senses that which is sensible. Rather, having become more than a human person, one looks on sensible objects in a spiritual way, as images of invisible things, and the forms they present are as if without form and figure."[27]

If this, briefly stated, constituted the approach of hesychasm to imagery, the iconographic creations inspired by it could not help but attribute a fundamental role to light.

That light whose value is eminently spiritual enlivens Theophanes' *Virgin* with an inexhaustible life.

From a Deësis—St. John the Baptist

"It can be said of one who practices contemplation that it is as if he is standing near the spring which Scripture says poured forth from the earth at the beginning, so abundantly that the whole earth was watered by it. Whoever approaches this spring will marvel at the unending stream of water that does not cease to gush forth and diffuse itself. One can never claim to have seen all this water, for who can see what is still hidden in the womb of the earth? So, as long as one remains beside this gushing spring, one always remains at the beginning of his contemplation of the water.

"The same is true of one who contemplates the unlimited divine beauty: everything one discovers is constantly revealed as totally new, and one never stops desiring more, because what is awaited is even more magnificent and more divine than what has already been seen."

St. Gregory of Nyssa, *In Cantica*, *Hom.* XI; PG 44, 1000AB

From a Deësis—St. John the Baptist

> "Of all the children born to women,
> there has never been anyone greater
> than John the Baptist."
>
> *(Mt 11:11)*

St. John the Baptist, who recapitulates in himself the long waiting of the people of Israel, is the first to point Jesus out as the desired Messiah and to participate in the mystery of the hiddeness and humiliation of this Servant of Yahweh who asks him for baptism. Having become the first martyr for Christ, he possesses, like all martyrs, the power of intercession.

As it clearly appears in the Old Testament concerning Jeremiah the Prophet, who had died centuries earlier, the capacity for intercession was already recognized by men of God: "This is a man, who loves his brothers and prays much for the people and the holy city—Jeremiah, the prophet of God" (2 M 15:14). And the Church could do nothing but only confirm this role, so the Book of Revelation presents: "the four living creatures prostrated themselves before him and with them the twenty-four elders; each one of them was holding a harp and had a golden bowl full of incense which are the prayers of the saints" (Rv 5:8).

After the Blessed Mother, John the Baptist, "friend of the Bridegroom," deserves a place of honor. Just as in the Book of Revelation the prayers of the saints are inserted into the liturgy of heaven, so the prayers of the Mother of God and of the Precursor will consist above all in asking that the participation of believers in the earthly liturgy, in the body and blood of the Lord, be for them a source of grace and mercy.

In the present icon, a work of one of Andrei Rublev's disciples, inner unification and spiritual clairvoyance are marvelously reflected in the noble, refined, and delicate features of the Precursor's face.

The singular resemblance of John's features to those in icons of Christ illustrates the true meaning of the Russian adjective *prepodobnyi,* meaning "resembling most closely" which defines human sanctity: the saint is one who resembles God, in Christ.

16. St. John the Baptist (Deësis).

The prayer which the Eastern Church addresses to John the Baptist may be helpful for better understanding his gaze and gestures: "May your hand, O Baptist, which touched the head of the Lord, and which pointed out to us that he was the Savior, be extended towards him in our favor, in virtue of that ample assurance you enjoy, since according to his own testimony you are the greatest of all the prophets. And may the eyes which beheld the Holy Spirit descending in the form of a dove be turned towards Christ, O John the Baptist, so that he may grant us his grace."[28]

From a Deësis—St. Paul

"*Just as the sun is the same substance throughout, possessing no inferior or imperfect parts, but is entirely radiant with light, and is all the self-same light..., so the soul which has been fully illumined by the ineffable beauty of the glory of the light of Christ's face and made to share perfectly in the Holy Spirit, and judged fit to become the dwelling and the throne of God—this soul now becomes all eyes, all light, all countenance, all glory, and all spirit because Christ thus prepares it, carrying it, directing it, sustaining and leading it, and, in this way, adorning and beautifying it with spiritual beauty.*"

St. Macarius the Egyptian, *Hom. 1;* PG 34, 451B

From a Deësis—St. Paul

> "Because of the supreme advantage
> of knowing Christ Jesus my Lord,
> I count everything else as loss."
>
> *(Ph 3:8)*

T he first believers to be placed in the Deësis at the sides of the Mother and of St. John the Baptist are the apostles, the "pillars of the Church," especially Peter and Paul, with their unmistakable traits: the same that appear in their most ancient representations on Roman medallions of the third and fourth centuries, but now interpreted and transfigured by the skill and interior vision of the iconographer.

Thus Rublev, in the Deësis of Zvenigorod, portrayed the Apostle Paul totally illumined by a light emanating from within: the icon's so-called "proper" light, bestowed by the presence of the Holy Spirit.

This light blends in with another light from outside, which shines from the left, where Christ is seated. But even this is a spiritual light, of which the Psalm speaks: "Fix your gaze on Yahweh and your face will grow bright" (Ps 34:5). The light, then, shines from both within and without, yet it is the same light, transforming the one who contemplates it so that he becomes "all eyes, all light, all countenance."[29]

Through the shape of the head and forehead, that spherical form which in all cultures symbolizes divine perfection and which was such a favorite of his, Rublev emphasizes visually the primacy of the spiritual that is so characteristic of Pauline thought.

The face of the Apostle, in which is reflected the face of Christ (cf. 2 Co 4:6), stands out in its warm ochre colors against the watery tints of the garments, rendered almost transparent by the soft and gradual highlighting typical of Rublev's hand. This sun-like glow is countered by a precious blue, pure and intense, made from the powder of lapislazuli.[30]

Strength is here wedded with sweetness in an extraordinary harmony of lines and colors which again suggests the teaching of St. Paul: "The fruit of the Spirit is love, joy, peace, patience, kindness, goodness, trustfulness, gentleness and self-control..." (Ga 5:22).

17. The Apostle Paul (Deësis of Zvenigorod).

From a Deësis—The Archangel Michael

"*The lightweight wings of the angels symbolize the absence of any earthly attraction, a pure and total thrust toward the heights, devoid of any heaviness. The luminous and incandescent garment signifies the divine form with the symbol of fire: that power of enlightenment which the celestial intelligences derive from their being assigned to dwell in heaven, the very domain of light. The staff they carry indicates royal power, sovereignty and that rectitude with which they bring everything to completion.*

"*Scripture affirms that the angels participate in the divine joy over the repentance of sinners: in fact, they experience a tranquil and truly divine happiness, a joy full of goodness and without envy in providentially watching over and helping in the salvation of all who turn to God.*"

Dionysius the Areopagite, *De Hier. Cael.;* PG 3, 334A, 339A

From a Deësis—The Archangel Michael

> "Are they not all ministering spirits,
> sent to serve for the sake
> of those who are to inherit salvation?"
>
> *(Heb 1:14)*

D ionysius the Areopagite liked to call the Eucharist the "sacrament of reunion"—"synaxis"—because the Eucharist brings about in the most perfect way the union of persons with God and with each other, besides the reunification of the individual's own being; it is the gift *par excellence* of the unifying Father's goodness.

In the Old Testament as well as in the New, the role of angels could not help but be involved in this unifying will of the Father of light. The angels, purest contemplators of God's glory, render to him a perfect cult of adoration and praise, singing a hymn to his holiness, and he communicates to them a share in his mysterious fire. The earthly liturgy, therefore, is modeled on their heavenly one, as so admirably expressed in the Byzantine liturgy: "We, who mystically represent the cherubim as we sing to the life-giving Trinity the hymn 'Holy, Holy, Holy,' now lay aside every earthly care."

However, the celestial beings also maintain an active role in preparing, sustaining, and guiding human beings, as is said, for example, of the Archangel Michael, "the great Prince, defender of your people" (Dn 12:1) and in presenting their supplications to God.

The *Archangel Michael* silently transmits this message: he is one of the perfect servants, totally transparent, of the Most High God. Everything in this composition of Rublev is clarity, lightness, and harmony: there are no hard lines nor harsh spots; everything is expressed in parabolic curves and recurring colors, like the head band that completes the arc with the deep blue of the tunic.

More eloquent than anything else however, is the unspoken word of the face; designed two-dimensionally, it "opens out"[31] towards the spectator, bearing witness to a total openness resulting from knowledge and love.

18. The Archangel Michael (The Deësis of Zvenigorod).

St. George

"The glory that the saints now possess in their souls will cover and reclothe their naked bodies and snatch them up to heaven. And finally, with our body and soul we will rest eternally with the Lord in the kingdom....

"The world of Christians is indeed a different world: their food, their style of dress, their entertainment, their communion with each other, their way of thinking. That is why they are the strongest people. They receive their strength in the intimacy of their souls from the Holy Spirit. For this reason, in the resurrection, even their bodies will be worthy of the eternal goods of the Spirit, and they will be united to the glory of him whom their souls have already experienced here and now."

St. Macarius the Egyptian, *Hom. V,* PG 34, 516CD

St. George

"For it is not against human enemies
that we have to struggle,
but against the principalities and the ruling forces
who are masters of the darkness in this world,
the spirits of evil in the heavens."

(Ep 6:12)

I n the spaces of the iconostasis between the doors of the sanctuary—
under the architrave on which is found the Deësis—were placed
icons of local saints to whom the church was dedicated or who received particular veneration. Among these saints, one of the best
known and loved in Russia was certainly the great and glorious martyr,
St. George.

The extremely rich symbolism linked to the figure of St. George suggests a series of fundamental themes rooted in the most profound human
and Christian experience: the horseman appears in all cultures as signify-
ing the mastery of the spirit over the senses, and his resplendent white horse
expresses the majesty and beauty which then follows.

The Judeo-Christian tradition could not fail to offer a particularly favorable terrain for the development of this theme. And it found one of its
clearest and most vigorous expressions in this ancient devotional icon—not
created solely for an iconostasis.

The dragon-serpent which emerges from the grotto—a symbol of pri-
mal chaos and of vital potentialities not yet formed—is the personification
of the "beast" within us that the Christian is obliged to kill, as well as of
the Evil Force which one must vanquish to live according to the spirit.

Even the bare mountain underlines this necessity of ascending to the
heights, towards the absolute that, for the Christian, is the love of the Father manifested in the Son and experienced in the Spirit. This pole of
attraction and source of outpouring of grace is symbolized by the hand bestowing a blessing in the upper right-hand corner of the icon.

On the striking red background, typical of the school of Novgorod, the
immaculate white horse stands out like a space of absolute light. The general impression of lightness and movement is conveyed by the extreme

19. St. George.

elegance of the lines and by the overlapping of some parts of the figure over the frame.

However, it is a movement where balance reigns. The descending diagonal line of the lance thrust into the dragon's throat offsets the ascending line of the horse's body, reinforced higher up by the parallel line of the flowing mantle. Similarly, the perfect curve of the horse's brilliant neck corresponds to the irregular opening of the dark cavern.

The Icon of the Twelve Feasts

"My brothers, it is a wonderful thing to move from one feast to another, from one prayer to another, from one celebration to another.... However, the graces of a festive celebration are not limited only to the moment, nor are their splendid rays extinguished as soon as the sun goes down; these graces are always available to the soul who desires them. They exercise continuing power on those whose minds have been illumined and who meditate day and night on the sacred Scriptures....

"The liturgical celebration sustains us in the afflictions which we encounter in this world. Through it, God grants us that joy of salvation which enhances fellowship."

St. Athanasius, *Ep. V;* PG 26, 1379-1380

The Icon of the Twelve Feasts

"This is the stone which you, the builders, rejected
but which has become the cornerstone.
Only in him is there salvation;
for of all the names in the world given to men,
this is the only one by which we can be saved."

(Ac 4:11-12)

As was the case with the Deësis, which was reproduced in numerous more or less detailed portable models, so the Feasts of the Lord were portrayed in a unique composition of miniatures made accessible outside the sacred precincts of a church for prayer and contemplation by the faithful.

The Twelve Feasts celebrated with particular solemnity in the Eastern Churches are, in chronological order: the Birth of Mary, her Presentation in the Temple, the Annunciation, the Nativity of the Lord, his Presentation in the Temple, the Theophany (the Baptism of the Lord), the Transfiguration, the Entry into Jerusalem, the Ascension, Pentecost, the Dormition of the Mother of God, and, finally, the Rediscovery and Exaltation of the Cross.

It is immediately noticeable that the feast of the Lord's Resurrection is not included in this selection. Easter is indeed always the "feast of feasts," the feast par excellence, around which revolves the entire liturgical calendar, weekly as well as annual. The icon of the Twelve Feasts presents this central truth visually by placing in its center panel the Paschal Mystery in its fruits: the redemption of mankind and the glorification of Christ. In the lower scene, the risen Christ descends into hell to liberate Adam and Eve; on the right Christ rescues Peter from the water into which he was sinking; this is one of the most ancient paradigms of "salvation." In the central scene we have the apparition of the angel to the women who are carrying aromatic spices, and the door of paradise, guarded by one of the seraphim, is now wide open. The figure of the resurrected Christ, who is the Redeemer, as emphasized by the cross in his left hand, is duplicated and exalted, in the upper dome, as the Judge and Lord who sits in the heavens, being served by the angels.

20. *The Twelve Feasts of the Church.*

93

The scene of the crucifixion forms no part of the Twelve Feasts. For Christ's death as such can scarcely be "celebrated" as a "feast" because in itself it is a negative, destructive event. The death of Christ can be considered a mystery only insofar as its salvific significance is fulfilled—and this occurs only with the Resurrection.

The Conception of St. Anne

"Because it was to come about that the Virgin Mother of God should be born of Anne, nature did not dare to anticipate the seed of grace; it remained deprived of fruit so grace would produce its own. That firstborn of all women had to be born so that she could give birth to the Firstborn of all creatures, who 'exists before all things and in [whom] all things hold together' (Col 1:17).

"O happy couple, Joachim and Anne! To you all creatures are indebted, because through you creation offered the most pleasing of all gifts to the Creator, namely, the chaste Mother who alone was worthy of the Creator."

St. John Damascene, *In Nativitatem Mariae*, 2; PG 96, 663AB

The Conception of St. Anne

"Shout for joy, barren one who has borne no children!
Break into cries and shouts of joy, you who were
never in labour!"

(Is 54:1)

From the fourth century on, the creation of a liturgical cycle of the Lord's feasts was linked to the popularity of pilgrimages to the Holy Land, to the sites of Christ's life. The creation of this liturgical cycle was a work of primary importance for the Church in Jerusalem and, in particular, for the monks of St. Saba in the Kidron valley, who made use not only of Scripture but also of the creative spirituality contained in the apocryphal writings. These became a font of inspiration that would be amply reflected in many iconographic themes linked to liturgical texts.

One of the most ancient apocryphal writings, dating from the second century, was the *Protoevangelium of James,* which narrated the life of the Blessed Virgin Mary up to the birth of Jesus. It is precisely from this book that we learn the name of Mary's parents, Joachim and Anne, as well as the tradition that Anne was sterile and was enabled only in her old age to conceive the daughter who was destined to gladden all humanity.

Spiritual sensitivity, in fact, could not help recognizing in the conception of this New Eve the fulfillment of that mystery of free election and fruitful grace proclaimed throughout the entire Old Testament by the victory of God over sterility: "The whole universe celebrates today the conception of Anne, brought about by the will of God. She conceived the one who in her turn conceived, in an ineffable manner, the Word."[32] The eminence of the daughter, by reflection, renders the mother great: for that reason, from the basilica in Jerusalem that stands on the traditional birthplace of Mary, devotion to St. Anne spread rapidly throughout the Christian world.

According to the apocryphal account, Mary's conception by her mother Anne was announced by an angel to the two elderly people separately. This conception was portrayed by the embrace of Joachim and Anne in front of the Golden Gate in Jerusalem. Even though this kind of scene was used in

96

21. The Conception of St. Anne.

secular art to depict the conception of an illustrious person, this symbol of union, in itself eminently spiritual, became for Christians an allusion to Mary's total purity. This purity referred not merely to the holiness of life of the future Mother of God; it pervaded her entire existence from the time of her own conception. This is what Christianity taught from the beginning, expressing it figuratively in the symbolic language of the apocrypha.

Already by the second century, with its parallel between Mary and Eve, enriched by the one between the Son and the Mother intimately associated in the work of salvation, St. Irenaeus provided an extremely precise and fruitful doctrinal content in his reflection on the mystery of Mary: "...the Lord...derived from her, descendant of Adam, the likeness of this first creature. It was entirely fitting and proper that Adam should find his fulfillment in Christ so that mortality could be absorbed in immortality. Similarly, Eve should find her fulfillment in Mary, so that a Virgin should intercede for a virgin, that the virginal disobedience should be canceled out by the deeds of virginal obedience."[33]

This parallel between Eve and Mary appears continually in the thought of the Fathers of the Church as the key to understanding the absolute, new beginning that was realized in the Virgin Mary. It was a marvelous new beginning on which the holy Metropolitan of Crete Andrew (seventh century), author of some of the most beautiful liturgical poems in honor of the Mother of God, fixed his gaze: "The body of the Virgin is a field in which God himself labored, the first fruit of the race of Adam to become divinized in Christ, an image completely resembling primordial beauty, the clay modeled by the hands of the divine Artist."[34]

The present icon, the *Conception of St. Anne,* is from the school of Novgorod. Probably because its theme was in itself so intimate, the scene is in an indoor setting, as indicated by the ample draperies extending between the two buildings. In Byzantine art this constitutes the conventional sign of being indoors.

The buildings of Jerusalem depicted in the background seem to open out and move towards the viewer. The space is not in an illusory depth, but "over here," surrounding the one who is contemplating it. Because the sacred image has a "salvific content" for humanity, its source is in God and its vanishing point is the human soul. This, in short, is the significance of the "reverse perspective," an aesthetic method characteristically employed in icons of Byzantine inspiration. Such a convergence of the perspective lines towards the viewer is evident from the graphics outlined in the accompanying figure.[35]

To emphasize still more the timelessness of the message, Joachim and Anne are clearly placed on this side of the background, standing on a small

platform, as if they are outside of the story, in an absolute "present." Linked to the joyous beginning of the Redemption, their icon becomes at the same time the icon of conjugal love which, generously included in God's eternal plan of salvation, regains all its original dignity.

The Annunciation

"The source of incorruptibility, our Lord Jesus Christ, did not come into this world through a marriage. By the mode of his Incarnation he intended to show this great mystery: that only purity is capable of accepting God when he asks to enter. In fact, what took place within the body of the inviolate Virgin Mary through the perfect divinity of Christ which shone in the Virgin herself, occurs also in every soul who remains a virgin according to the spirit. It is not that the Lord becomes physically present anymore, but he comes to dwell in us spiritually, bringing the Father with him."

St. Gregory of Nyssa, *De Virginitate;* PG 46, 324B

The Annunciation

"When the completion of the time came,
God sent his Son, born of a woman,
born a subject of the Law,
to redeem the subjects of the Law,
so that we could receive adoption as sons."

(Ga 4:4-5)

As is well known, the proclamation at the Council of Ephesus of Mary as "the Mother of God," *Theotókos,* resulted in a veritable explosion of Marian devotion in the East. During the sixth century various feasts linked to Mary were instituted. These were the Birth of Mary, the Annunciation, the Presentation of the Lord, and the Dormition. With the institution of two other feasts, the Conception and the Presentation of Mary, more than a century later, liturgical practice consecrated the ancient desire of the Christian people to observe the closest possible analogy between the Mother and her Son.

From the sixth century on there existed in the East two iconographic models of the annunciation. The more ancient one, also influenced by apocryphal writings, pictured Mary sitting and spinning, but drawing back, troubled and frightened by the apparition of the angel. The other model, inspired by the Byzantine concept, showed her standing "as if receiving a royal command,"[36] a wise and prudent virgin, carefully appraising the words of the angel: "She did not immediately give in to joy nor accept what she was being told; rather, troubled, she asked what the greeting meant."[37]

In the second model the position of Mary's right hand could vary: when the palm was turned outwards, it signified reservation and an initial refusal; however, when it was turned towards her chest, showing the back of the hand, it indicated her acceptance.

There probably does not exist any more masterful and integral representation of the annunciation than the very ancient one (twelfth century) from an iconostasis in the region of Novgorod,[38] in which the two persons, larger than life in the Byzantine fashion, stand out, solid and monumental, against a golden background.

22. The Annunciation.

The only indication of surroundings is the small platform beneath the feet of the Virgin Mary; this suffices to show that the scene is taking place on earth. With restrained strength, the messenger, clothed in red, white, and gold garments, richly draped to indicate his closeness to the divine Source, reveals the staggering weight of his message: "Today is the dawn of our salvation and the manifestation of the eternal mystery."[39]

In marked contrast, the Virgin is calmly and completely enclosed within her cherry-red *maphórion,* covering a sober blue garment. She inclines her head slightly in a movement of welcome, attentive to the words of the angel. Her large eyes, angled ever so slightly downwards, giving them an air of sweetness, are not fixed on the angel but rather on the inner vision of the mystery being realized in her.

A smile full of trust and grace plays upon her face. Both the inclination of the head and its features resemble those of the Mother of God of Vladimir, but what a profound difference between the two in the degree of conscious knowledge suggested! While the "Vladímirskaya" anticipates with a kind of spiritual comprehension the degree and weight of her mission as Mother of the Savior, this "Virgin of Ust'jug" is living through the magic and wonder of beginnings. Incredibly young and delicate, she recalls the Bride from the Song of Songs: "Fountain of the garden, well of living water, streams flowing down from Lebanon!" (Sg 4:15) She embodies the dream of what Woman was when she came from the hands of her Creator.

Up to this point, her right hand has been occupied in weaving thread—to symbolize her insertion into time and human history—but now this hand has ceased to labor and has been raised up to the level of her heart, where the Incarnate Word appears. It is as if time had stopped for an instant at the moment the Most Pure said "yes" to her Creator; henceforth, time will be divided into a "before" and an "after."

The thread also has another, more specific meaning: according to the apocrypha, it was the purple spun by Mary for the veil of the Holy of Holies when she was living in the Temple, and which prefigured the humanity that the Mother would "weave" for her Son. With a very beautiful image, St. Andrew of Crete compared the Virgin herself to the royal purple: "The purple which colored the 'fabric' of the Word in his ineffable Incarnation was his Virgin Mother whom we glorify."[40]

Solemn, in blessing, the figure of the Christ Child averts every temptation to consider him a child generated according to the flesh; Mary, Mother *because* she remains a Virgin, has become the dwelling place of her Lord conceived through the work of the Holy Spirit.

This divine, rather, Trinitarian dimension of the occurrence is reinforced by the lunette up above—appearing for the first time in this icon—depicting God the Father as "the Ancient of days" from Daniel's vision, with his throne supported by seraphim. From the Father's hand, a ray symbolizing the descent of the Holy Spirit is directed towards the bosom of the Virgin—there where Emmanuel appears.

This time, it is liturgical texts which greatly influenced the icon's composition. For example, there is the extremely profound text of St. Andrew of Crete found in the solemn Vespers of the feast: "Ineffable is the nature of this humiliation, ineffable this way of conceiving. An angel functions as the servant of this wonder; the womb of a Virgin receives the Son; the Holy Spirit covers her with his shadow; the Father in heaven above is well pleased—and this union is accomplished according to a common will."[41]

The Nativity

"*The mystery of God who became man, the divinization of the human-ity assumed by the Word, the revelation of the mystery of God, the humiliation of the divine nature—these are the gifts which Christ has be-stowed on us. The coming of God among men, like a splendid light and as a clear and visible divine reality—this is the great and marvelous gift of salvation into which we have been introduced.*"

St. Andrew of Crete, *In Nativitatem Mariae;* PG 97, 804B-808A

The Nativity

"Look, I am making
the whole of creation new."
(Rv 21:5)

T he task of iconography in the Church is to express the theological and spiritual content of revelation in a summary fashion through images. This explains the surprising richness of this icon of the nativity, in which events distinct from one another in time and place, as well as symbolic figures, appear together to point out the different dimensions of the mystery being celebrated.

In this masterpiece from the school of Rublev which succeeded in unifying the various narrative elements, the principal iconographic model concerning the Mother-and-Child pair is the one that was used from the sixth century on. Up to that point Mary had been shown seated with the child on her knee, in accordance with an authoritative teaching of St. John Chrysostom: "She herself laid the Child in the manger and later placed him on her knee."[42]

This attitude was a way of showing that Mary had in no way suffered when giving birth and reflected the very real preoccupation at that time to indirectly affirm her perpetual virginity. Once her inviolate integrity was no longer being doubted, Mary was pictured stretched out like any other woman who had just given birth, to emphasize the human concreteness of the nativity.

The scene showing the bathing of the Child indicates a double influence. From the apocryphal gospel of Matthew comes the inclusion of the midwife as a witness to Mary's virginity, while the bathing of the newborn was an element carried over from pagan art. Since there was no reason for any purification in the case of the Incarnate Word, the bath became a figure of baptism, so the basin, as in the present icon, took the form of a baptismal font.[43]

The first pattern that strikes the viewer when looking at the icon as a whole is its triple horizontal subdivision, around the principal scene of the nativity.[44]

23. The Nativity.

In the bottom strip of the icon are represented the earthly aspects of the great event. On the one hand, its concrete reality: the nurse and the bath of the newborn. On the other, its being outside the normal laws of human generation. The figure of St. Joseph is used to transmit this message both by his distance from the Mother-and-Child figure (according to classical iconographic models, this was intended to represent Joseph's non-participation in the conception of the Child),[45] and by the suggestion of how difficult it was for human thought, hampered by its own innate material-ism, to enter into the mystery. The identity of the person facing St. Joseph is unknown—he could be a figure from pagan mythology, or Isaiah the Prophet, or a devil tempting him,—in any case, he is the "exteriorization" of this difficulty which can become a temptation.

In the icon's middle strip is depicted the first manifestation (Epiphany) of the Incarnate Word: to the angels and the shepherds. The mystery is present and as such even the Mother is contemplating it. Stretched out in repose like any other woman who has just given birth, she yet remains the Most Holy Queen, the Mother of God, whom the red carpet interwoven with gold encloses within a cocoon of glory.

The Baby wrapped in swaddling clothes anticipates the Man who will be wrapped in a shroud and laid in the tomb. His head is located precisely on the vertical axis of the whole icon, clearly marked by the divine ray of light. Precisely around this tiny Son of Man will be unleashed the titanic battle which is already lurking behind him, in the pitchblack cave.

Everything will be decided around him because, in reality, he is the axis of the entire world. The traditional figures of the ox and the ass (here a horse, since, in Russia, the ass was unknown) symbolize that creation which "is waiting with eagerness for the children of God to be revealed" (Rm 8:19), and which has already recognized in this Babe the Creator and Savior.

The top section depicts the manifestation of the Lord to the Magi, which the East celebrates along with the feast of the Nativity. This theophany is cloaked in silence: the star is the sign of God's presence. The angels adore the sign of salvation in its eternal actuality, while the Magi, the first to make the pilgrimage to Bethlehem, and representing everyone who will follow, seem to be drawn out of time towards the divine ray, in whose light they are completely immersed.

The vertical movement built into the design of this icon unifies the three segments into a summary vision of the plan of salvation in accordance with the thought of St. John Chrysostom, for whom Epiphany, Easter, and even Pentecost are already contained within the Nativity.

110

The mountainous terrain guides the eye from the bottom towards the star. This movement encompasses the dark grotto and is reinforced by the fiery red diagonal of the Mother, which, in marked contrast with the blackness of the cave, seems to burn from within like a large, tranquil flame. It is as if the iconographer wished to express by means of this contrast an unspeakable joy: the joy of humankind conscious of being able to offer to its Creator and Redeemer something besides its own misery and obscurity, namely, the One who is "more venerable than the cherubim and incomparably more glorious than the seraphim": She who is the honor of the human race.

From above, light falls upon the rocks in transparent cascades; it makes the tree trunks and branches sparkle; it adorns the edges of the fountain and turns the water from the jug into liquid gold. The effect of the Pasch of the Lord is the gift of the Spirit, his penetration into cosmic and human reality.

Theophany: The Baptism of Christ

"Jesus consecrated baptism when he himself was baptized. Who without great impiety can despise baptism if the Son of God himself was baptized? He was baptized, however, not to receive the forgiveness of sins (he was totally removed from sin), but rather, although free from sin, he was baptized in order to bestow divine grace and dignity on those who would be baptized.

"According to Job, there was a dragon in the waters that swallowed up the Jordan. Therefore, since the heads of the dragon had to be crushed, by descending into the waters, Christ bound the force of evil so we would be empowered to walk on serpents and scorpions."

St. Cyril of Jerusalem, *De Baptismo III;* PG 33, 441AB

113

Theophany: The Baptism of Christ

> "...and suddenly the heavens opened...."
>
> *(Mt 3:16)*

f the feast of the Nativity, and its icon, draw our attention to the unfolding in time of the mystery of Redemption—the feast of the Baptism, instead, presents the contemplation of this same mystery in its eternal beginnings; it is "theology."

The very moment when Jesus "fulfilled all righteousness," or rather, manifested his acceptance, as Yahweh's servant, of the way of humiliation and annihilation, coincides with the messianic anointing conferred upon him by the Father: "This is my Son, the Beloved; my favor rests on him" (Mt 3:17). This was the first theophany of the Trinity and it revealed the eternal source of God's plan.

It is in this perspective that the "theology" of baptism is to be found: the mystery of God, Trinity of love, could only be revealed when the "sole Righteous One" manifested his total loving obedience to the Father. When the "first-born of all creation" (Col 1:15) voluntarily descended into the waters of death, the heavens opened. The feast of the Baptism of the Lord, therefore, celebrates the beginning of the new creation, vivified by the presence of the Holy One of God.

All this is suggested by this very beautiful icon with its pronounced vertical composition. Between the harsh, almost chiseled, mountains, the dark mass of the Jordan appears as if in a narrow gorge. Into this abyss, this "black ocean, liquid tomb," truly descended the "most beautiful of all the sons of men," bestowing a blessing and clearly delineated in the classic proportions typical of the Greek school, full of serene majesty. At his feet the rocky walls widen into a kind of cavern filled with water, which reminds us of the dark cavern from which the risen Lord will draw out the ancient fathers.

A strict parallel exists between the descent into the Jordan and the descent into hell. In the Hebrew conception, the waters of the abyss with their destructive force represented the powers of evil, so in both cases, Christ enters into the dominion of Satan to vanquish him. The descent into the

114

24. The Baptism.

115

water prefigures the ultimate defeat of Satan and the salvific illumination that would be ushered in with the Paschal mystery, according to the incisive expression of St. Cyril of Jerusalem: "Descending into the waters, Christ chained the evil one."[46]

The words of Isaiah would come true: "That day Yahweh will punish, with his unyielding sword, massive and strong, Leviathan the fleeing serpent" (Is 27:1). Nevertheless—and this is precisely the message of the epiphany at the Jordan—this "unyielding sword," paradoxically, consists in the total humiliation of the Incarnate Word: "You have crushed the head of demons by bowing your head before your precursor, and, descending into the wave, you have lighted up the universe to glorify you, O Savior, the light of our souls."[47]

From the opened heavens erupts the divine ray, a visual equivalent of the Father's voice, penetrating deeply into the space between the mountains as into the depths of the earth; in the ray is depicted the dove representing the Spirit. Along this vertical line which unites heaven and earth, the mystery of the Holy Trinity appears in its eternal order, which is the salvation of humanity: from the Father, by means of the Son, in the Holy Spirit, to all the living.

Amazed, but ready to serve, the angels are present at this incomprehensible humiliation of the Incarnate Word which prefigures his death. Meanwhile, John the Baptist apologetically performs the action ordered by Christ. The axe laid to the root of the tree announces that the last days have begun; access to the kingdom has been reopened with the condition of following the way marked out by the servant of Yahweh: "Hear him!"

Below, represented by the allegorical figures of the Jordan and the Red Sea, the waters which previously had been the dwelling place of monsters recognize the Lordship of the Word Incarnate and, sanctified by his presence in a marvelous reversal of the situation, themselves become a vehicle of salvation for humanity.

This was the significance of the memorial cross which the Christians of Palestine erected in the waters of the Jordan at the traditional spot where Jesus was baptized. At times, this appears in icons of the Baptism of the Lord.[48] In our icon, beneath Christ's feet, can be distinguished three stone steps which serve as a base. To clarify the presence of the fish swimming around his legs: the little fish, *pisculus,* is actually the symbol of the baptized Christian who, liberated, can now freely swim in the waters of life— that life which proceeds from the Body of the Lord, matter totally permeated by the Spirit.

The Transfiguration

"Let us raise our eyes towards the heights and peacefully receive the beneficial ray of Christ, who is the absolute good, who transcends every individual good: may his light elevate us to the divine workings of his goodness. Is it not he himself who, having created everything, desires that every creature live in close contact with him and share in a communion with him insofar as possible?"

Dionysius the Areopagite, Ep. VIII; PG3, 1086D

119

The Transfiguration

"And all of us, with our unveiled faces
like mirrors reflecting the glory of the Lord,
are being transformed into the image that we reflect
in brighter and brighter glory;
this is the working of the Lord who is the Spirit."

(2 Co 3:18)

About the middle of the fourth century, St. Helena had a basilica constructed on Mount Tabor to commemorate the Transfiguration. Around that same time pilgrimages started going to Sinai, the holy mountain, with the burning bush as a point of reference—in accord with the tradition of Moses' vision.[49]

The site of the great theophany in the Old Testament could not help but be a tremendous means of grasping the incredible changes that had taken place: the passage from Sinai to Tabor, from the dark cloud to the light of the Transfigured One, from the unattainable transcendence of the living God to the divinization of human nature through the mediation of the Word Incarnate.

Irenaeus is found commenting on these words of Yahweh: "for no human being can see me and survive...[but] here is a place near me. You will stand on the rock, and when my glory passes by, I shall put you in a cleft of the rock and shield you with my hand until I have gone past" (Ex 33:20-22). He explained: "Two things were indicated by this: first, that a person is incapable of seeing God, but secondly that through the wisdom of God, one will see him at the end standing 'upon the rock,' that is, in his coming as man. For this reason he conversed with him face to face on the mountain in the company of Elijah, as the gospels report, thus fulfilling the ancient promise."[50]

So, when the Monastery of St. Catherine was built in those holy places (sixth century), the first known representation of the Transfiguration of the Lord appeared in the mosaic of the apse. Its composition was so perfect that the iconographic scheme would never be substantially changed: Christ, resplendent with light, surrounded by a circle of glory and flanked

25. *The Transfiguration (order of the Feasts from the Church of Volotovo).*

by Moses and Elijah, is being contemplated by the three apostles, prostrate or falling down at his feet.

Especially clear here is the affinity between the vision and the image. Just as the act of vision—or of contemplation—takes in multiple data simultaneously, so its figurative expression, by its nature obliged to prescind from the dimension of time, is able to present an extremely rich and multiform reality, which imposes itself upon us immediately in its totality.

This can be verified by looking at this icon of the Transfiguration from the school of Novgorod (fifteenth century). The one who contemplates it takes in the whole message at once,—the actuality of the mystery—and must then proceed to analyze it in terms of the symbolic language of the linear and chromatic composition.

The basic structure consists in: a large circle—expanding, since it becomes progressively lighter—placed over a triangle whose very regular structure is outlined by the rays that issue from the circle's axis, which is formed by the white figure of Christ.

The circular movement of the cloud of glory is accompanied and amplified by the external contours of the two figures of Moses and Elijah; but the folds in their robes also suggest a horizontal line which cuts across the center of the cloud, forming a kind of cross. In the lower part of the icon the contour set in motion by the falling of the apostles is contained in the arc of a circle indicated by the three rays.

The first message conveyed by this structure is that the fullness of life (the circle), manifested as light radiating from the figure of Christ does not remain enclosed in itself but includes all creation in its movements, especially humanity. This encounter, an absolute source of happiness for all creatures, takes place on the mountaintop (the triangle), which is the universal symbol of the meeting place between heaven and earth, the point of the outpouring of divine goodness, and, inversely, the point of convergence for all human efforts to ascend towards God.

The figure of Christ in composite continuity with the mountain depicts the symbolic equation established by St. Paul: "that Rock was Christ" (1 Co 10:4). He himself, the Mediator between God and humanity, is the Mountain, the absolute meeting place between God and his people.

In this icon of the Transfiguration, the news of the sorrowful journey is downplayed. What is suggested, rather, is the first day of the new creation called to share in the light and beauty of God: "Look, I am making the whole of creation new" (Rv 21:5). The entire scene, in fact, is bathed in the sunlight of high noon, without any shadows. The deep, warm, active

122

colors—from yellow-orange to red-purple—are in marked contrast with the cold range of various shades of green[51] and show nature at the peak of its vitality and luxuriance. It is the great day, the day without sunset, the summer solstice. In the circle of glory, which is also the circle of time, the luminous Christ stands as the vertical line of the zenith and of the eternal solstice.

The Last Supper

"The Pasch that Jesus desired to share with us was what he would suffer: through his suffering he freed us from suffering, through his death he conquered death, and through visible nourishment he procured for us his immortal life. Behold the salutary desire of Jesus; behold his entirely spiritual love for us: to show the signs as signs, and in their place, to give his own sacred body to his disciples: 'Take and eat, this is my body; take and drink, this is my blood—the new Covenant, shed for you for the remission of sins.' If he desired more to suffer than to eat, this was to liberate us from the suffering incurred by eating."

From a Homily Inspired by "On the Passover" by St. Hippolytus of Rome, SC 27, p. 174

The Last Supper

"Before the festival of the Passover,
Jesus, knowing that his hour had come
to pass from this world to the Father,
having loved those who were his in the world,
loved them to the end."

(Jn 13:1)

The Last Supper of Jesus with his apostles on the vigil of his passion is at the same time a historical event: the meal with the traitor present, and also a mystery beyond time: the institution of the Eucharistic Sacrament. From its very first representations (sixth century), this double significance has inspired two distinct iconographic themes.

The first theme, more common in the West, depicted the apostles gathered around Jesus, pondering with intense emotion the tragic announcement of the betrayal.

The second theme, very dear to Byzantines, illustrated the liturgical-sacramental act of the communion of the apostles. In the eleventh century it appeared in the hemicycle of the apse in churches, and later, on Russian iconostases, above the royal door (the central door leading into the sanctuary). Christ the Priest, placed in the center, distributes the bread and wine to the apostles, divided into two groups.

Byzantine art clearly preferred the second theme, but it continued to portray the historical Supper in a composition that evolved equally in both East and West, passing from the semicircular Hellenistic table to a round table. From the viewpoint of the onlooker, Christ is seated at the extreme left, in what was considered to be the place of honor. John's leaning profoundly towards Jesus allows Peter, flanked traditionally by Andrew, to occupy the second place next to the Master, while the placing of Judas varies. Most of the time, as in the present icon from the northern school, Judas follows immediately after these three and is shown reaching for a morsel of food, in accordance with the gospel text: "Someone who has dipped his hand into the dish with me will betray me" (Mt 26:24).

126

26. The Last Supper.

If one should ask what is the source of the great sense of warmth, intimacy, and peace which flows over the viewer of this icon in successive waves, the answer confirms once again the symbolic role of the colors and the structural composition.

The spectator must be confronted with the mystery of the Last Supper: that mystical banquet, both spiritual and sacramental, where Jesus Christ, in whom "in bodily form, lives divinity in all its fullness" (Col 2:9), became one in being with us, as Gregory Palamas wrote, so that we in our turn might be transformed in him. How better to symbolize this theme of deification, which from St. Irenaeus on constitutes the fundamental point of thought in the Eastern Church, than to focus everything around the circular structure of the table, while, at the same time, creating a movement upwards towards heaven?

Because of the inverse perspective, the tabletop is shown upright so the spectator can see its full dimension, and it forms the true and ideal center of the composition, emphasized even more by the whiteness of the tablecloth. The apostles are spread around it in a circle; their garments, in complementary reds and greens, contribute to the overall atmosphere of harmony and tranquility.

The figure of the Lord, the only one represented in full body, while remaining part of the circle, is both raised up and somewhat set back. This privileged position reveals itself as the point of arrival for a great movement. This movement forms an S, starting from the outstretched hands of the apostle who is seated in the lower left hand corner—standing out much more than Christ because of his position and colors—and proceeding along through the other apostles, with its upper curve indicated by the position of John's hands raised in prayer. The movement follows through in Jesus' act of blessing, itself an integral part of the ample rising curve of his entire figure.

The rigid line formed by Judas' downward movement does not succeed in breaking up the harmony of the composition, because to the left of this line, the artist did not simply continue the edge of the table but visibly raised it up, increasing the table's surface and creating a strong counter-movement.

The suffused evening light falls on the ample, embroidered tablecloth, vibrates in the various subdued reds of the garments, mounts up behind the Lord, moves along the luminous pillar of the building that is right behind Jesus' shoulders, runs along the rose-red drapery hanging above, and continues to shine with great intensity inside the little cupola which crowns the pillar on the right.

Anchored firmly in the stability of the composition's lower segment, the two vertical architectural structures accent the ascending movement

128

found in the center of the circle. At the same time, they introduce an element of breaking away and changing levels: the repose of the mystical Banquet is not yet that of the Eighth Day, when the King "will do up his belt, sit them down at table and wait on them" (Lk 12:37), but it is its earthly anticipation.

The Crucifixion

"He did not die involuntarily, nor was his death merely the result of violence; he offered himself of his own free will. Listen to what he himself said: 'and as I have power to lay it down so I have power to take it up again' (Jn 10:18). Thus he proceeded of his own free will towards his passion, happy to undertake a work so sublime, filled with joy over the fruit that his act would produce, namely, the salvation of humanity. He was not ashamed of the cross because it procured the redemption of the world. Yet it was not just any nondescript man who suffered thus; it was God made man, and, as a man, he was fully intent on obtaining the victory through obedience."

St. Cyril of Jerusalem, *Cat.* XIII; PG 33, 779BC

131

The Crucifixion

"Jesus too suffered outside the gate
to sanctify the people with his own blood.
Let us go to him, then, outside the camp...."

(Heb 13:12-13)

T he only theme of Christian iconography in the first three centuries
was that of the salvation and eternal life reserved for those who
believe in Christ. First appearing in baptistries and cemeteries,
these Christian themes found expression in harmony with the
iconographic tradition, already developed in the Jewish milieu, of portraying
scenes dealing with outstanding divine interventions in favor of God's faithful
people: Noah saved from the flood, the three young men preserved in the midst
of the fiery furnace, Daniel rescued from the lion's den, and so on. To these
Old Testament examples of salvation, Christians naturally added those of the
New Testament intimately connected with the life of Christ: the great healings
of the paralytic, of the man born blind, of the woman with the hemorrhage, and
the raising of Lazarus from the dead. The absolutely new historical event of
salvation through Christ's paschal death and resurrection, however, was recalled
only indirectly, for example, by depicting the sacrifice of Isaac; or symbolically
by using pictures of the anchor, the lamb, or the pierced dolphin.

The very lack of any preceding iconography explains why this event,
and the scene of the crucifixion in particular, appeared only later in the
repertoire of images—at the end of the fourth century. This was not so much
because of the scandalous and infamous nature of this type of execution; it
simply reflected the characteristic conservatism of religious iconography. In
reality, only the incredibly strong impetus brought about by the discovery
and veneration of the Holy Places in Palestine—in particular the cult of
relics of the True Cross—proved capable of sustaining the creative process
for an iconography of the passion.[52] Like all other ancient iconographic
models regarding the person and life of Christ, this one too assumed the
connotations of a theophany right from the beginning.

The athletic body of the crucified Christ was painted in an erect position, with no sign of having undergone any suffering; most of the time it
was clothed in a brief linen tunic (the *colobium*). Christ is already dead

27. The Crucifixion.

133

because blood and water are flowing from his pierced side, but his open eyes are those of the living One "that never close." Christian artists thus avoided the cruel and brutal aspects of the scene and presented it as a theophany of Christ the Lord; they expressed symbolically the truth professed by the Church of the two natures—human and divine—of the Incarnate Word: on the cross Christ as a man really died; but as God he continued to live.

The common belief of the times that the lion slept with his eyes open, coupled with the identification of Christ as the Lion of Judah (cf. Rv 5:5), helps us understand the particular theophany inherent in this image: "While the lion sleeps in his den, his eyes remain open according to Solomon in the Song of Songs: 'I sleep, but my heart is awake' (Sg 5:2). In the same way the body of my Lord sleeps upon the cross while his divinity keeps vigil at the right hand of the Father. For the fact is that 'he neither sleeps nor slumbers, the guardian of Israel' (Ps 121:4)."[53]

Centuries later, after the pressures from christological heresies had subsided, the contemplation of Christ's sufferings on the cross were no longer portrayed "in a manner contrary to nature," but rather "according to the natural human form."[54] No longer was Christ shown alive, erect, and triumphant, but rather, naked and dead, with his body bent to indicate the spasms of suffering.

In the Byzantine world, though, in spite of this fundamental change, the crucifixion scene remained immersed in an atmosphere of great nobility, where the sentiments of sorrow always yielded first place to the contemplation of the mystery.

This is what emanates from this Russian icon painted at the end of the 1300's, heavily influenced by the Byzantine art of the Palaeologus period. A sovereign equilibrium reigns over the entire composition: the cross is solidly planted in a rocky cone intended to represent Golgotha and stands out in a space which is cut in two by the walls of Jerusalem in the background. The slight forward inclination of the Mother is prolonged in the curve of the Son's body, while the void created thereby is filled by the contrastingly bent form of the apostle. The heads of all three figures are equidistant from each other, while the two angels above further accentuate the stability of the entire structure.

The same balance characterizes the emotions conveyed by this icon. The ancient gesture of sorrow—resting the cheek on the hand—here, rather, suggests contemplation and is only applied to John. The Mother continues to be she who intercedes. The angels veil their faces, overwhelmed at the incomprehensible humiliation of the Lord of life. What stands out above all,

however, is the peace of the majestic, and at the same time, delicate body of the Crucified, to which the curve of pain adds greater lightness and elegance.

"I see him crucified, and I hail him as King," St. John Chrysostom wrote.[55] The icon expresses this regal character through the unique brown-ochre color harmony of both the figures and the cross, which are rendered solemn and close at hand by the gilded lightness of the background. The watery reflections on the cloth draped around Christ's hips, on the tunics of Mary and John, and on the rocks of Golgotha help to dispel any suggestion of heaviness.

Blood spurts from Christ's side and flows from the wounds of the nails because, as Origen explained, the New Adam who went to sleep on the cross "was not like other dead men, but manifested from the depths of death signs of life in the water and the blood and thus was called a new kind of dead man."[56] Already illuminated, the skull of the old Adam is the first to receive the bath of Redemption.

135

A Redemption which extends to the entire universe and which finds its most complete symbol in the three dimensions of the Byzantine cross. The transverse arm of the cross, as well as its footboard, indicate the fourfold extension of earthly space, while the vertical axis points to the life-giving meeting between heaven and earth.

The cross of Christ is a cosmic cross that embraces the entire world in order to recreate it. As St. Irenaeus explained so beautifully: "Through the Word of God everything is brought under the influence of the redemptive work; the Son of God, through the blessing he bestowed, has stamped the sign of his cross on all things. It is he who illuminates the heights, that is, the heavens; it is he who penetrates the depths of the lower regions, he who stretches over the long distance between east and west, he who joins together the immense space between north and south—he it is who calls all men everywhere to the knowledge of the Father."[57]

The Descent into Hell

"The sacred rays of Christ's light shine, the pure torches of the pure Spirit arise, and the celestial treasures of divinity and glory are revealed; the dark and immense night has been swallowed up, the gloomy shadows have been destroyed in this light, and the dark phantom of death has returned to the shadows. Life is extended over all beings and every creature is filled with a great light. The Sun of suns occupies the heavens and he who was 'before the morning star,' greater than all heavenly bodies, immense and immortal, the great Christ shines more brightly than the sun upon all created things.

"This is why, for all of us who believe in him, a new day of light has begun, long, eternal, not to be extinguished, the mystical Pasch, celebrated figuratively by the Law and definitively fulfilled by Christ."

From: *A Homily Inspired by "On the Passover" by St. Hippolytus of Rome*, SC 27, p. 116

The Descent into Hell

> "Wake up, sleeper,
> rise from the dead,
> and Christ will shine on you."
>
> *(Ep 5:14)*

T he most ancient images of the Resurrection (third century), based on the gospel account, were those of the indirect witnesses of the event: the women at the tomb, Mary Magdalene's dialogue with the angel, and Thomas touching the bodily signs of the Lord's passion. Only towards the end of the first Christian millenium did anyone dare, for the first time, to picture Christ in the act of rising from the tomb; however, this theme was never taken up in the East.

There, in fact, another theme was solidly established, inspired by the images of imperial art, in which the victorious sovereign was depicted in the act of raising up—that is, of "liberating" from the "tyranny" of their leaders—the kneeling figures representing the conquered peoples.

These compositions were well adapted to the truth of faith, dating back to the earliest preaching by the apostles, that Jesus "descended into hell." This truth expresses the reality of Christ's death as a man, and at the same time his triumph over it: "He is the one who was not abandoned to Hades, and whose body did not see corruption" (Ac 2:31).

Christ's definitive victory over death carried with it an equally total liberation of humanity imprisoned by the power of death. With the reviving or raising up *(anastasis)* of Adam—this is the oldest name for this image—and of all the just who lived before the era of salvation, the history of the human race began afresh with the New Adam: "He is the Beginning, the first-born from the dead..." (Col 1:18).

Mentioned in the most ancient Eucharistic prayers and included very soon in the Creed, while later it was the subject of a dramatic and picturesque description in the apocrypha of Nicodemus, the Descent into Hell was also the summary theme of baptismal catechesis. Every catechumen could, in fact, recognize himself in that Adam for whom Christ descended into hell to lead him "out of the darkness into his wonderful light" (1 P 2:9).

138

28. The Descent into Hell.

An ancient "Homily on Holy Saturday," therefore, placed on the lips of Christ addressing Adam the very same words of the baptismal invocation used by the apostolic Church: "I am your God, who for you became your son. For you and for those who had their origin in you, I now speak and in my power I command those who were imprisoned: Come out! To those who were in darkness: Be enlightened! To those who were dead: Arise! You I command: Wake up, you who sleep! Rise from the dead!"[58]

This icon of the Descent into Hell is from the church of Volotovo near Novgorod; it proclaims this Easter message in a wholly unmistakable fashion.

In the great diagonal burst of light which comes from the illuminated mountain on the right, Christ is shown dynamically in the act of descending, as dazzling as a flash of lightning against the dark background of the halo of glory. At the same time he seems to be in an opposite movement, that of rising, almost being pulled powerfully upwards, drawing with him those he came to liberate.

The entire composition was conceived so as to convey this double, simultaneous movement. Thus, while the victorious dynamism of the figure of Christ is emphasized by the static pose of the two groups of people at his side, this latter inactivity, in turn, is no longer total because the sudden appearance of the One who is Life has aroused everyone from their ancient torpor.

The broad curve of Adam's figure reaches towards Christ the Savior as if bonded to him by Christ's strong grasp on his wrist. On her side, Eve, the Mother of all the living—represented in perfect color-complement to Adam—is ready to be raised up by the Lord. The hands of David, Solomon, and John the Precursor are extended toward him in prayer, while the mountain behind them resumes the curve of Adam's profile. Even the victorious cross, which functions as a kind of ray within the circle of glory, is placed slightly to the right of the vertical axis.

But it is probably on the illuminated mountain, in continuity with the flowing robes of the risen Lord, that the true key to the double movement can be found. In fact, through the effect of inverse perspective, the light falls, bouncing off of the enormous stone steps and being absorbed by the figure of Christ; it is refracted by the now useless prison instruments strewn at the bottom. But the convex curve of the mountain above, itself a product of the inverse perspective, creates an optical effect whereby the lines which include the mass of moving light seem to diverge again, opening out towards the infinite Light.

The Ascension

"*Since he took upon himself completely the entire 'image' (of God), and by shedding 'the old man,' he changed it into the 'heavenly man,' so now this image combined in him ascended with him to heaven. At the sight of this great mystery of a man thus ascending with God, the Powers cried out with joy to the heavenly hosts: 'Lift up your heads, O gates! And be lifted up, O ancient doors, that the king of glory may come in.' The heavenly hosts, in turn, witnessing the unheard-of prodigy of a God-man cried out in reply: 'Who is this king of glory?' And again those who were questioned replied: 'The Lord of hosts, he is the king of glory...the Lord, strong, valiant, and mighty in battle.'*

"O mystical choir! O spiritual feast! O divine Pasch, you descend from heaven to earth, and you return from earth back to heaven!"

From: *A Homily Inspired by "On the Passover"* by St. Hippolytus of Rome, SC 27, pp. 186-188

The Ascension

"I am with you always;
yes, to the end of time."

(Mt 28:20)

During the first three centuries of the Church's history, the memory of the "glorious Ascension of the Lord" was closely linked to that of his Resurrection. In fact, it signified the ultimate antithesis of the descent of the Servant of Yahweh. "O marvelous Easter!" exclaims an ancient *Homily on Easter.* "Life that rises out of the tomb, and healing that issues from the wound, resurrection that comes out of the fall and ascension that springs from the descent [into hell]."[59]

Later on, when the Ascension became the subject of a specific commemoration, it was first celebrated together with Pentecost. Then—at Antioch already from the middle of the fourth century—its celebration was definitely established on the fortieth day after Easter, in conformity with the account contained in the Acts of the Apostles.

These various stages were certainly not arbitrary expressions. After having perceived the mystery of the Easter Resurrection in its unity—Pentecost, or the fiftieth day of Easter, was in fact considered a temporal extension of the one feast—the Church's reflections gradually distinguished the various elements, making them the object of specific celebrations.

Thus, was recognized the intrinsic bond between the Ascension event and the contemplation of the most interior and hidden aspect of the mystery of the Church: the Church who lives in the presence of the Lord Jesus, glorified and seated at the right hand of the Father, the Lord of history who will return at the end of time; the Church who is conscious of being indissolubly linked to him in that humanity in which he ascended into heaven.

It is a completely interior aspect of reciprocal, unchangeable presence which St. Gregory of Nyssa expressed in the most beautiful imagery: from that of the lost sheep carried on the shoulders of the Shepherd to that of the wedding in which "the Bridegroom coming from the nuptial chamber united himself to us (who resembled a virgin who had given herself to idols), after having restored our fallen nature to its virginal integrity."[60]

29. The Ascension.

145

This theme of restored integrity—always linked to Easter—could not but recall next to Christ the New Adam, Mary the New Eve, the Virgin Spouse, figure and prototype of the Church.

Even the choice of an iconographic model was naturally affected by this progressive development of thought.

The earliest representation was, in fact, quickly abandoned; it depicted a silhouette of Christ walking up a mountain and extending his right hand towards the divine hand appearing in the heavens (fourth and fifth centuries). Besides obscuring to a certain degree the image of Christ's divine power, it focused upon a moment relatively insignificant to the content of the mystery.

The definitive model, which appeared in the sixth century, exhibited profound changes. It is a frontal composition divided into two sections: above, Christ, immobile in his glory being supported by angels; below, on the vertical axis, Mary, the Mother of God, flanked by two angels and surrounded by the apostles. Despite the fact that the Gospels and the Acts of the Apostles make no mention of it, the early Christian community was profoundly convinced that Mary had been present at all the important moments in the life of her Son. This conviction even found some mention in liturgical texts: "It was fitting that she who, as your mother, suffered more than anyone else during your Passion, should be filled to overflowing with joy at the glorification of your flesh."[61]

Thus, instead of a merely external representation of the event, the content of the mystery being comtemplated was translated into images.

This is what emerges from this icon of the Ascension painted by one of the disciples of Andrei Rublev in the fifteenth century, the most splendid period of Russian art, when no secondary elements had yet intruded to blur the transparency of the message.

Slightly inclined—in relation to the vertical axis—the elegant form of the Virgin in an attitude of prayer stands out dark against the funnel of light formed by the angels, who are pointing to heaven.

She alone, who is full of grace, has a halo like theirs, the sign of participation in the divine life. She alone looks straight ahead, while the apostles are either looking up to heaven or at her. She alone, in fact, through her luminous faith, continues to see the Lord Jesus Christ, whom the cloud has hidden from the gaze of the apostles and on whose golden garments is now reflected the glory of the Word of God.

She who conceived him in faith and who is called *Platýtera,* greater than the heavens, because her womb has carried him whom the whole universe could not contain, will in her turn be completely contained in him

in his Second Coming (indeed she already is). The eye of the viewer certainly notices that the shape of the light around the Virgin Mother which opens up towards the top, matches that of the glorious cloud. The resulting rhombus form symbolizes the union of heaven and earth, the overcoming of the spiritual/material dualism in a harmoniously achieved unity.

But all this still takes place in time, and history, affected from now on by the constant intervention of the glorified Lord. The wise orchestration of all the elements in this composition imparts to this icon a broad movement of rotation in a clockwise direction. The glorious circle is a sun-like wheel which turns, and the extended right arm of Christ, reinforced by the slight displacement of his position in relation to the vertical axis, indicates the direction of the movement.

Even the angels who support the glory share in this movement: the one in red, on the right, is "heavier," the one in green, on the left is "lighter."

The same effect is achieved on the earth by the two groups of apostles: those on the right are motionless, while those on the left are straining toward the heavens.

It is the same as the apparent movement of the universe: from west to east, from darkness to light. This is also the invisible movement of the life of the Church: always present to her Lord, always longing for his Coming. "The Spirit and the Bride say, 'Come!'...come, Lord Jesus" (Rv 22:17, 20).

Pentecost

"This is the Spirit whom, by means of the prophets, the Lord promised to pour out in the last days upon his servants, so they would receive the gift of prophecy. For this reason, the Spirit also descended upon the Son of God, become son of man, growing accustomed, along with him, to dwelling in the human race, to being at home among people, and to living in God's creatures, fulfilling in them the will of the Father and renewing them from the old man to the new life of Christ.

"Luke narrates that this Spirit, after the Ascension of the Lord, came down on the disciples at Pentecost, bringing both the will and the power to introduce all nations to the life and revelation of the New Testament."

St. Irenaeus of Lyons, *Adversus Haereses*, III, 17; PG 7, 929A

Pentecost

"Send out your breath and life begins;
you renew the face of the earth."

(Ps 104:30)

The first representations of Pentecost which came from Syria and Palestine had the same structural composition as those of the Ascension: the fire of the Holy Spirit descends upon Mary, standing in the midst of the apostles. However, with the gradual understanding of the special significance of Pentecost as a reflection on the apostolic mission of the Church, the iconographic formula was destined to change also.

Recourse was had to the classic model of the collective portrait,[62] already widely used in early Christian art, in which a group of wise men were shown seated in a semi-circle around their master. Such an arrangement, utilizing the symbolism of the circle, was well adapted to express the unity, equality, and communion among the members of the apostolic college gathered around Christ, the head of the Church. Whether in the end Christ was actually visually depicted, or whether his place was left empty to attest to his invisible presence, changed none of the significance.

On the other hand, the same structure had already been adopted in the interior architecture of cathedral churches, in both East and West. The clergy occupied seats in a semi-circle—the *synthronon* in Greek—around the bishop, who occupied the central place reserved for Christ. This explains why the iconography of the councils—which reflected the actual seating arrangement of the council fathers—resembled the iconography of Pentecost: the model was the same.

The newer style of portraying Pentecost spread from Cappadocia to Byzantium and was then adopted throughout the entire Christian East, although, there always remained some iconographers who, in conformity with the account in the Acts of the Apostles, depicted the Virgin Mother in the central place. The basic scheme of composition was integrated by a number of elements still very noticeable in this Russian icon of the Descent of the Holy Spirit, which visually translate an extraordinarily rich reflection on the mystery of the Church.

30. The Descent of the Holy Spirit.

What stands out to those viewing this icon, is the predominant shape of the arch. The fact is that the refusal of Byzantine art to depict the artificial perspective of the third dimension meant that depth would be projected upwards, so that a concave space would assume the shape of an arch.

In reality, there are three arches in this icon, one inside the other; they are typical Byzantine arches, tall and narrow. The highest of these arches results from the optical flattening of the curve of the apse of the church in which Pentecost takes place. We no longer find ourselves in the intimate, closed room of the Last Supper, but rather, in the public place of the manifestation of the faith and its proclamation to the world. Sharply highlighted by decorative elements, this upper arch forms a lunette in the center of which the viewer is supposed to "see" the figure of Christ, presiding invisibly over the assembly of his apostles.

The second arch corresponds to the semicircular seating of the apostles. The smallest arch is formed by the frame of the outside door, in which appears the figure of the Cosmos, an allegorical personage borrowed from pagan iconography representing the order of the created world (Gr. *Kosmos,* order).

This composition in its entirety thus coincides with the basic structure of the temple—the terrestrial cube surmounted by the celestial sphere—itself a "dynamic image of the dialectic between the transcendent celestial sphere to which we naturally aspire and the terrestrial sphere in which we actually find ourselves and in which we realize we are travelers on a journey to be carried out from this time forward thanks to the help of signs."[63]

In this way, the icon of Pentecost expresses the mystery of that living temple which is the Church, the privileged and unique place for this journey from earth to heaven.

But there can be no ambiguity regarding the active principle of this journey: the barrier of nature can be truly and definitively overcome only in virtue of a gift from above. That is why the ascending movement of the arches, already restrained by the dark void which opens up behind the figure of Cosmos, and also by the slight divergence of the two architectural structures, seems to be turned upside down by the presence, in the upper part of the icon, of the large dark hemisphere and its rays, a symbol of the divine transcendence.

"O that you would rend the heavens and come down!" (Is 64:1) At Pentecost, that historical event which is perennially renewed in the bosom of the Church, the ancient desire of humanity was granted. Dionysius the Areopagite explained that the secret of that Darkness, which is the effect of the most brilliant but inaccessible Light on human eyes, is manifested

and communicated by means of the triply luminous Ray of the gratuitous and salvific revelation which God, Father, Son, and Holy Spirit makes about his own personal being.

"In thy light do we see light!" (Ps 36:9) Everything comes to fulfillment in the outpouring of the Spirit. As St. Basil explained: "In the illumination of the Spirit, we will see the true Light that enlightens every person who comes into the world."[64] That light without any shadow flows through the golden areas of the icon as purest water.

The presence of St. Paul in the assembly of the apostles, to the right of the empty place reserved for Christ, points out that this assembly is to be considered not as an historical moment of the first Pentecost, but rather in its role as proclaimer of the Word. In fact, the apostles hold the resplendent scrolls of the revealed Word, already proclaimed to the whole world.

The figure of Cosmos, composed and illuminated, stands out against the darkness of chaos and sin. By contrast, the concave line of the white material he is holding in his hands forms a perfect receptacle for the flames which are descending from above. He is not only the personification of cosmic harmony; he prefigures the new person restored to his primordial beauty by the Spirit.

This, then, reveals the total mystery of the Church, predestined, before the creation of the world, to show forth the splendor of the divine beauty manifested in Christ.

The Dormition

"No, you were not merely like Elijah 'taken up to heaven'; you were not like Paul, transported to the 'third heaven.' Rather, you reached the very throne of your Son, in immediate vision, in joy, and you remain at his side with great and unspeakable security. For the angels and for all the powers that rule the world, you are ineffable happiness; for the patriarchs, endless delight; for the just, inexpressible joy; for the prophets, perpetual exultation.

"A blessing for the world, sanctification for the whole universe; comfort in suffering, consolation in tears, healing in sickness, a port in the storm. For sinners, pardon; for the afflicted, benevolent encouragement; for all those who invoke you, an ever ready assistance."

St. John Damascene, *In Dormitionem* I; PG 96, 717AB

The Dormition

> "Thus he chose us in Christ
>   before the world was made
> to be holy and faultless before him in love."
> *(Ep 1:4)*

T he conviction that the body of Mary, the Virgin Mother, did not undergo the corruption of the tomb goes back to the first Judeo-Christian communities. The most ancient nucleus (second-third centuries) of the apocrypha entitled *Dormitio Mariae,* contains the account, rather fantastic in its language but unambiguous as far as content is concerned, of Mary's bodily assumption into heaven.

It is to be noted, furthermore, that there was an uninterrupted tradition in Jerusalem regarding the place of Mary's burial (or temporary interment) as being in a tomb in Gethsemani over which the Emperor Theodosius I had a church erected near the end of the fourth century. And it was precisely from the celebration held on August 15th in this ancient center of Marian devotion that the date for the feast of the Dormition of Mary was derived. It extended throughout the entire East in the sixth century, and was adopted soon after by the Latin Church, also.[65]

Having been developed only from the ninth and tenth centuries on, the iconography of the Dormition reflects the imaginative account contained in the *Dormitio,* whose text had soon become an integral part of the celebration of the feast, and whose faith content had been deepened by the Fathers of the Church, in particular, St. John Damascene. The arguments in favor of Mary's bodily assumption which recur in the patristic writings had already been found, although expressed symbolically, in the writings of the first centuries. They included: the dignity of the body of the Most Pure Virgin, the "dwelling place of the Lord"; her participation in the glorious life of her Son, symbolized by the fact that, according to the apocryphal account, Mary spent three days in the tomb, watched over by the apostles, until the Lord came, accompanied by angels, to take her body away; her intimate union with her Son's work of salvation and, as a consequence, the importance of her intercession.

31. The Dormition.

157

All of these themes are reshaped by the theme of life, an incorruptible life of which the *Theotókos* was the privileged receptacle; from this came the dominant symbolism of light. It pervades this ancient, moving invocation to Mary: "We pray to you, O Mary, light and mother of light, Mary, life and mother of the apostles, Mary, golden lamp which bore the true lamp, Mary our queen, appeal to your Son...."[66] The same theme is woven into the liturgical texts of the feast: Mary is "the candelabra of the inaccessible light," "the Mother of inexhaustible light," "the bright lamp of the immaterial fire (of the Word Incarnate), the golden censer on which the Lord reposes like embers." She herself "delivers her brilliant soul into the spotless hands of the one who without human seed took flesh in her."

The theme of light is the constant key to understanding this marvelous Russian icon. It comes from the school of Tver' (fifteenth century), and was inspired by one of Rublev's models. Significantly, it is called "the Blue Dormition."

Wrapped in her dark *homophórion* the Virgin is laid out on a piece of fiery red material, which strikingly recalls the one on which the Mother was resting in the icon of the Nativity; it seems to light up the faces of the apostles leaning over her. They are all present, showing the sadness of parting. Peter is at the head of the bed and Paul at its foot. John, depicted as an old man, lays his head next to the Virgin on the cushion just as he laid it on the Lord's bosom. Behind the apostles, who have been transported to Jerusalem by angels in order to be present at the passing of Mary (see the upper part of the icon), are two bishops of the early Church, disciples of St. Paul: St. Dionysius the Areopagite, bishop of Athens, and St. Timothy, bishop of Ephesus. Then there are individuals representing the Christian people.

The eyes of all converge towards the center to that body which, as the liturgy declares, was "the bearer of God and the source of life." The departing Mother finds herself enveloped by the veneration and human tenderness of the Church.

However, this descending movement is overcome by the strong upward thrust of the pointed arch. In contrast to its intense blue enriched with transparent green which embraces the entire length of the couch, stands the gilded vertical figure of the Savior. On his face one reads the strength and determination of the Risen One, the one who has vanquished death.[67] The Lord of glory, clothed in light, carries up to heaven the small white figure which represents the soul of the Most Pure Virgin. Even the distinctive upward rays which surround him indicate the re-ascending of the Son who came to take his Mother.

"While the very lintels of heaven were raised and the angels were

158

singing to you, Christ welcomed you, O Mary, as the treasure of virginity—
you whom the cherubim in glory serve and the seraphim in happiness
glorify."[68] The angels of the glorious procession, painted all one color, also
form the heavenly portals; their lighted candles are the same shape as the
one which, placed over the Virgin's head, signals the beginning of the icon's
upward movement.

In the continuous dialogue of color between the area of the couch and
that of the arch is found the fulcrum of this composition. The brightness of
the red-orange and the deepness of the blue-green attain their maximum
degree of intensity precisely because these two complementary tones are,
at the same time, to be found at opposite poles of the hot-cold spectrum.
The flame rises up towards the depths of the sky, and the sky unceasingly
revivifies its ardor. This suggests that the ascending force which carries our
Lady to glory has its origin in her immaculate body, and—following the

curve of the arch held up by the vertical axis expressed in the figure of Christ—vanquishes death, penetrating the sphere of the divine life symbolized by the color blue.

Nevertheless, the elevation-glorification of the Mother of God does not mean the closing of the earthly chapter of her existence. The iconographer suggests this by the expanding movement which characterizes the upper part of the icon. In fact, while the two edifices on the sides attenuate somewhat the convergence of the arch, everything else is widened and definitively opened up by the concentric semi-circles of the apostles transported by the angels.

At the center of this particular movement, against a background of threefold glory, there appears the small, seated figure of the Mother of God, surrounded with light, an almost hidden marvel of this icon. Incredibly humble and simple she extends her open hand in a gesture of welcome and of giving: "In your maternity you remained a virgin, in your dormition, you have not abandoned this world, O Mother of God. You were transferred to life, you who are Mother of the Life, and you rescued our souls from death through the power of your intercession."[69]

This is the song of joy which resounds during the entire month of August in the liturgy of the Eastern Church.

The Trinity

"When the Spirit is in us, the Word from whom we receive him is also in us, and in this Word there is also the Father, so thus is realized what has been said: 'We will come to him and make our home with him.' Where there is light, in fact, there is also its splendor; and where there is splendor, there is likewise its efficaciousness, and its splendid grace.

"Just as grace comes to us from the Father through the Son, so we actively share in this gift only through the Holy Spirit. Thus, having become participants, we enjoy the love of the Father, the grace of the Son, and the communion of the Holy Spirit."

St. Athanasius, *Epistula I ad Serapionem;* PG 26, 599BC

The Trinity

"We have recognised for ourselves,
and put our faith in, the love God has for us.
God is love,
and whoever remains in love remains in God
and God in him."

(1 Jn 4:16)

From the earliest centuries, Christian iconography attempted to represent the mystery of the Trinity, but of the many attempts to do so, only one withstood the test of time: the one depicting the episode of the Three Visitors at Mamre, who enjoyed the hospitality of Abraham. The Fathers of the Church soon considered this as prefiguring the mystery of the Trinity. In fact, the Baptism of Jesus, which is the first clear trinitarian theophany in history, did not sufficiently present the mystery of the three divine Persons equal to one another in every way.

The reproduction of the scene of the Three Visitors at Mamre, found in the churches of all Christendom from the fifth century on, preserved the realistic features of the episode. Abraham and Sarah were shown against the background of their tent; often a servant was shown killing a calf; and there was a well-furnished table with all its utensils. However, when in 1422 the holy monk and iconographer artist Andrei Rublev brought his *Trinity* to completion, it was immediately clear that the method of treating this theme had been radically changed, and changed to such an extent that in 1551 a council of the Russian Church declared that the *Trinity* of Rublev was "proto-revealed," that is, a symbolic image inspired by God himself.[70]

From what kind of spiritual roots did such a marvelous flower spring?

To seek a reply to this question, it is necessary to go quite far back in time. The Church's contemplation of the Trinitarian mystery soon acquired very precise formulations which had considerable spiritual consequences. Thus, for example, St. Irenaeus of Lyons had already intuited the way that brings Christians into the bosom of the Trinity: "Those who have taken on and bear the Spirit of God are led to the Word, that is, to the Son, and the Son receives them and presents them to the Father, and the Father renders them incorruptible."[71]

162

32. The Trinity.

For the Fathers of the Church, the science of God (theology) had as its object the mystery of the Trinity, however, never in the sense of an abstract speculation, but rather, as Evagrius expressed it, as the supreme and ultimate source of salvation and beatitude: "The kingdom of God is— knowledge of the Holy Trinity."[72] In itself, of course, the mystery of God is inscrutable. That is why, while assuming that the indispensable requirement for attaining the kingdom is the practice of love as described in the gospels, the Fathers of the Church, being great contemplatives, applied themselves to the search for the method of such knowledge.

They studied more deeply the meaning of the theophany on Sinai, when Moses, having ascended the mountain had seen the place of "the God of Israel beneath whose feet there was what looked like a sapphire pavement pure as the heavens themselves" (Ex 24:10). The Fathers explained that for Christians this "place" is inside of us. "Once the mind has divested itself of the old man and put on the new garment of grace, then, in time of prayer, it will perceive its own state as very similar to the color of sapphire—or of heaven—a state which Scripture calls the 'place' of God."[73] This state, which is the "place" of God, in reality coincides with the full manifestation of the divine image impressed on the person, who becomes similar to God. "When the spirit has been judged worthy to remain in contemplation of the Holy Trinity, it is then called God through grace, because it is looked upon as an image of the Creator himself."[74]

There is a profound, almost tangible concordance between this doctrine which for centuries has nourished monastic spirituality, and the *Trinity* by Rublev. The viewer should not think of it as an artificial representation of this mystery, but as the symbolic projection of a trinitarian experience analogous to that understood in the doctrine of the great spriritual writers.

Even to Rublev, immersed by the grace of God in the contemplation of the ineffable mystery, there must have appeared "in time of prayer...his own state very similar to the color of sapphire—or of heaven." And in that perfect image, "the 'place' of God," he must have seen reflected what is in itself totally hidden about the three divine Persons.

Thus what seemed impossible comes about: that we find ourselves in front of an image that is completely human and completely spiritual at the same time, in which matter has become the transparent vehicle of the Spirit. Here color is light, and line is movement. That movement which is the sign of life. Nor can we forget that light itself is a vibration and hence is also indicative of life.

The viewer who comes upon the *Trinity* of Rublev unexpectedly, catching sight of it from a short distance away in a room in a gallery, lit only by daylight from a side window, will have the unforgettable mem-

ory of an encounter striking for its beauty and its utter realism. The three life-sized figures seem to draw near, catching and submerging the viewer in a sea of beatitude. The dominant impression is brightness. The yellows, greens, and lilacs are very light and transparent. In the center, there is the resonant area of red-violet and of that incredible blue mantle of the central angel which reappears in the dress of the angel on the right. Is this not perhaps the very color of sapphire—of heaven—which is the "place" of God?

The movement which animates the entire composition proceeds from the angel on the right, is conveyed further by the inclination of the center angel, and, gathered in by the third angel, flows anew towards the right to conclude and perpetuate its ceaseless circular motion. Because they do not meet, the gazes of the three angels leave the interior space open to signify that the perpetual exchange and the communication of love between the Three Persons is a mystery of total interiority.

But something unforeseen happens precisely in the returning motion of the angel on the left: already pushed forward by the angel's erect position, the arch of the circle formed by the three heads is further expanded by the lines of the seats and the footrests which converge towards a point outside the icon, where the viewer is standing. And thus the closed sphere of the Three is dis-closed, and the mystery of their superabundant Life is manifested to the one who contemplates as infinite Love the large chalice formed by the side angels, and as Love bestowed, the cup which rests on the table.

Notes

1. Egon Sendler, *L'icône image de l'invisible,* coll. Christus n. 54, Desclée de Brouwer, Paris, 1981, p. 108.

2. Maximus the Confessor, *Mystagogia I;* PG 91, 668A.

3. This passage was determined by the influence of the architectural form of the central plan of baptistries and *martyria,* those chapels or other structures for prayer erected on the tombs of the martyrs or upon Holy Places related to the life of Christ (Cf. A. Grabar, *Martyrium: Recherches sur le culte des reliques et l'art chrétien antique,* Collège de France, Paris, 1946).

4. Athanasius, *Against the Pagans* 42; PG 25, 83B.

5. Cf. C. Capizzi, *Pantokrator (Saggio d'esegesi letterario-iconografico), Orientalia christiana analecta* 170, IOS, Rome, 1964.

6. Simeon the New Theologian, *Ethique III,* 325-330; SC 122, Paris, 1966, p. 415.

7. Champeaux-Sterckx, *Introduction au monde des symboles,* Collection Zodiaque, 1972, p. 101.

8. St. Gregory of Nyssa, *In Cantica,* Hom. XV; PG 44, 1093D.

9. St. Irenaeus of Lyons, *Adversus Haereses,* IV, 6, 6; PG 7, 989C.

10. St. Irenaeus of Lyons, *Adversus Haereses,* V, 16, 2; PG 7, 1167C.

11. For the significance of the composition of the Deësis, see "The Order of the Deësis," p. 65. The *Deësis of Zvenigorod* is certainly a work of Andrei Rublev, and takes its name from the place where it was discovered in 1918, near the Church of the Dormition in Zvenigorod. Only three out of the original seven figures of this work have come down to us: the central figure of *the Savior;* that of *St. Paul;* and that of *the Archangel Michael.* In a rather unusual way for this type of composition, these figures are depicted as busts.

12. Cf., Egon Sendler, *Les icônes de la Mère de Dieu,* in *Plamia,* n. 67, 1985, p. 11. As Fr. Sendler points out, in the Church of the Blachernae in Constantinople—built to house the precious relic of the Veil of the Virgin—the *Maphorion*—there was a fountain whose water flowed from two apertures in the hands of a "Praying Virgin" made out of marble.

13. André Grabar, *Iconographie de la Sagesse divine et de la Vierge,* in *Cahiers Archéologiques,* VIII (1956), pp. 259-261.

14. Fozio, *In dedicatione novae basilicae,* PG 102, 572B.

15. St. Irenaeus of Lyons, *Adversus Haereses,* V, preface; PG 7, 1120B.

16. Cf. S.I. Maslenitsyn, *Jaroslavian Icon-Painting,* Iskusstvo Publishers, Moscow, 1973, pp. 6-7.

17. Cf. Leonid Ouspensky, *Essai sur la théologie de l'icône dans l'Eglise ortho-doxe,* Paris, 1960, p. 96.

18. Cf. Konrad Onasch, *Icônes,* Geneva, 1961, *Dictionnaire de spiritualité ascé-tique et mystique* (DSAM), VII, 1237. art. *Icône.*

19. Hubert du Manoir, *Maria,* Beauchesne, Paris, 1949, Vol. I, p. 305.

20. Gregory Palamas, *In Dormitionem,* PG 151, 468AB.

21. Valentino Pace, *Pittura bizantina nell'Italia meridionale* (XI-XIV centuries) in *I bizantini in Italia,* Libri Scheiwiller, Milan, 1982, p. 474. See also: Kurt Weitzmann, *Studies in the Arts at Sinai,* Princeton University Press, Prince-ton, N.J., 1982, p. 75.

22. To come as close as possible to portraying the Invisible constituted the funda-mental motive of Byzantine art, as has been masterfully brought out by André Grabar. Cf. his study *La représentation de l'Intelligible dans l'art byzantin,* in *L'art de la fin de l'Antiquité du Moyen Age,* I, pp. 51-62, Paris, 1968.

23. Master Eckhart, *Traités et sermons,* Paris, 1943, cited by Jean Chevalier, *Dictionnaire des symboles,* Laffont, 1969, article "Virginité," p. 809.

24. Dionysius the Areopagite, *De Hier. Caeli* c. 3; PG 3, 164D.

25. From "Letter Written from Epiphanes the Wise to Cyril of Belozersk" (in Russian), quoted by G.I. Vzdornov, *Theophanes the Greek,* Iskusstvo, Moscow, 1983, p. 40.

26. St. Basil the Great, *In Psalmum* 44; PG 29, 400C.

27. Simeon the New Theologian, *Cat.* XIV; SC 104, Paris, 1964, pp. 213-215.

28. Prayer from Nones for the Vigil of Epiphany (January 5).

29. St. Macarius the Egyptian, *Hom.* I; PG 34, 451AB.

30. Egon Sendler, *L'icône...,* (Note #1 above), p. 219.

31. *Idem.,* p. 112.

32. *Kontakion t 4* from Morning Prayer for the Feast of the Conception of St. Anne (Dec. 9).

33. St. Irenaeus of Lyons, *Demonstratio apostolica* 33; SC 62, Paris, 1969, p. 85.

34. St. Andrew of Crete, *In Dormitionem;* PG 97, 1068, cited by Martin Jugie, *L'Immaculée Conception dans l'Ecriture Sainte et dans la tradition orientale,* Academia Mariana, Rome, 1956, pp. 107-108.

35. Precisely to help single out the principle parts of the icons' composition, even the following icons of the Feasts, which are more complex, will be accompa-nied by a similar graphic sketch.

36. *Mésaritès* 22, cited by Gabriel Millet, *Recherches sur l'iconographie de l'Evangile,* Editions de Boccard, Paris, 1960, p. 68.

37. St. John Chrysostom, *In Mat. Hom.* IV; PG 57, 45.

38. It is called *"The Annunciation of Ust'jug"* because, according to legend, its origin was the monastery of the *Velikij Ust'jug* in the extreme north of Russia.

39. Troparion t. 4 of the Great Vespers for the Feast of the Annunciation (March 25).

40. St. Andrew of Crete, Ode 9 t.1; Matins for Feast of the Conception of St. Anne (Dec. 9).

41. St. Andrew of Crete, Aposticha t. 4; Great Vespers for the Feast of the Annunciation.

42. St. John Chrysostom, *In Mat. Hom.* VIII, cited in G. Millet, *Op. cit.,* p. 99.

43. Cf. Louis Réau, *Iconographie de l'art chrétien,* PUF, Paris, 1957, Vol. II, pp. 220-223.

44. Egon Sendler, *"Icône de la Nativité"* in *Plamia,* n. 58, 1981, pp. 21-32.

45. André Grabar, *Christian Iconography—A Study of Its Origins,* Princeton Univ. Press, 1968, p. 130.

46. St. Cyril of Jerusalem, *Cat.* III, 11; PG 33, 441.

47. Stichera, t. 2 of the Great Vespers for the Feast of the Epiphany (January 6).

48. Cf. L. Réau, *op. cit.* p. 299.

49. Cf. John Galey, *Sinai and the Monastery of St. Catherine,* Stuttgart-Zürich, 1979.

50. St. Irenaeus of Lyons, *Adversus Haereses,* IV, 20, 9; PG 7, 1037C.

51. Cf. Johannes Itten, *Kunst der Farbe,* Otto Maier Verlag, Ravensburg, 1961.

52. Cf. A. Grabar, *Martyrium* II, *op. cit.,* pp. 257-259.

53. Text taken from the *Physiologus* cited by Alois Grillmeier, *Der Logos am Kreuz,* Munich, 1956, p. 84.

54. Michael Cerularius (eleventh century), cited by G. Millet, *op. cit.,* p. 399. The earliest examples go back to the eighth century and originated in a Palestinian milieu. Cf. K. Weitzmann, *The Monastery of St. Catherine at Mount Sinai— The Icons—*Volume One: *From the Sixth to the Tenth Centuries,* Princeton University Press, 1979, p. 61.

55. St. John Chrysostom, *De Cruce et latrone;* PG 49, 413, cited in Pietro Galignani, *Il mistero e l'immagine,* La Casa di Matriona, Milan, 1981, p. 171.

56. Origen, *Contra Celsum* II, 69; PG 11, 904, cited in Charles André Bernard, *Le Coeur du Christ et ses symboles,* Téqui, Paris, 1981, p. 53.

57. St. Irenaeus of Lyons, *Demonstratio apostolica* 34; SC 62, Paris, 1969, p. 87.

58. "In Sabbato Magno," *Hom.* II; PG 43, 461B.

59. Text taken from a *Une homélie inspirée du traité sur la Pâque d' Hippolyte,* SC 27, Paris, 1950, pp. 116-118.

60. St. Gregory of Nyssa, *In Cantica,* Hom. XI; PG 44, 997A, quoted in Jean Daniélou, *Platonisme et théologie mystique,* Aubier, Paris, 1944, p. 180.

61. Idiomele t. 4 of the Great Vespers for the Feast of the Ascension.

62. André Grabar, *op. cit.* (Note #45 above), pp. 69-70.

63. Champeaux-Sterckx, *op. cit.,* Note #4 above, p.131.

64. St. Basil the Great, *De Spiritu Sancto* XVIII; PG 32, 153B.

65. Cf. Bellarmino Bagatti, *Alle origini della Chiesa* II, Libreria Editrice Vaticana, Vatican City, 1982, p. 142.

66. Bellarmino Bagatti, *La Chiesa primitiva apocrifa,* Edizioni Paoline, Rome, 1981, p. 75.

67. Egon Sendler, *op. cit.* (Note #1 above), p. 56.

68. Ode 4 t. 1. of Matins for the Feast of the Dormition of Mary (August 15).

69. Troparion t. 1. of the Grand Vespers for the Feast of the Dormition of Mary.

70. Cf. Leonid Ouspensky, *La théologie de l'icône dans l'Eglise orthodoxe,* Cerf, Paris, 1982, pp. 265-266 (English text: *Theology of the Icon,* St. Vladimir's Press, Crestwood, N.Y., 1978).

71. St. Irenaeus of Lyons, *Demonstratio Apostolica* 7; SC 62, Paris, 1969, p. 41.

72. Evagrius of Pontus, *Capita Practica* III; PG 40, 1221D.

73. *Ibid.,* *Capita Practica* LXX; PG 40, 1144A.

74. *Ibid., Centurie* 5, 81, Frankenberg 355, quoted in DSAM II-2, col. 1782-1783, article "Contemplation."

Bibliography

Works of a general nature

Paleochristian and Byzantine art

Bellarmino Bagatti, *Alle origini della Chiesa,* 2 vols., Libreria Editrice Vaticana, Rome, 1981-1982.

Dictionnaire d'Archéologie Chrétienne et de liturgie, Paris, 1907-1953.

André Grabar, *Le premier art chrétien,* Gallimard, Paris, 1966.

André Grabar, *Christian Iconography—A Study of Its Origins,* Princeton University Press, 1968.

André Grabar, *Martyrium. Recherches sur le culte des reliques et l'art chrétien antique,* Collège de France, Paris, 1946.

Gabriel Millet, *Recherches sur l'iconographie de l' Evangile aux XIVe, XVe, et XVIe* siècles, Ed. de Boccard, Paris, 1960.

Kurt Weitzmann, *The Monastery of Saint Catherine at Mount Sinai—The Icons— Volume One: From the Sixth to the Tenth Century,* Princeton University Press, 1979.

Symbolism-spirituality-art

Charles André Bernard, *Théologie symbolique,* Téqui, Paris, 1979.

Champeaux-Sterckx, *Introduction au monde des symboles,* Zodiaque, 1972.

Jean Chevalier, *Dictionnaire des symboles,* Ed. Laffont, Paris, 1982.

Dictionnaire de spiritualité ascétique et mystique (DSAM)

Johannes Itten, *Kunst der Farbe,* Otto Maier Verlag, Ravensburg, 1961.

Heinrich Pfeiffer, *Gottes Wort im Bild—Christusdarstellungen in der Kunst,* Verlag Neue Stadt, München-Zürich-Wien, 1986.

Tomás Spidlík, *La spiritualité de l'Orient chrétien,* Pont. Inst. Orient., Rome, 1978.

Eugene N. Trubetskoj, *Icons: Theology in Color,* St. Vladimir's Press, Crestwood, N.Y., 1973.

Works of a specific nature

Theology of icons and iconographical art

Paul Evdokimov, *L'art de l'icône. Théologie de la beauté,* D.D.B., 1970.

André Grabar, *La représentation de l'Intelligible dans l'art byzantin in L'art de la fin de l'antiquité et du Moyen Age,* I, pp. 51-62, Paris, 1968.

Konrad Onasch, *Russian Icons,* Phaidon Press (E.P. Dutton), New York.

Léonide Ouspensky, *Essai sur la théologie de l'icône dans l'Eglise orthodoxe,* Editions de l'Exarchat Patriarcal russe en Europe occidentale, Paris, 1960 (English translation; *Theology of the Icon,* St. Vladimir's Press, Crestwood, N.Y., 1978).

Léonide Ouspensky and Vladimir Lossky, *The Meaning of Icons,* St. Vladimir's Press, Crestwood, N.Y., 1982.

Christoph Schönborn, *L'icône du Christ,* Cerf, Paris, 1986.

Egon Sendler, *L'icône, image de l'invisible,* D.D.B., Paris, 1981.

Art books

M.V. Alpatov, *Early Russian Icon Painting,* Iskusstvo, Moscow, 1974.

M.V. Alpatov, *Andrei Rublev,* Istituto Editoriale Italiano, Milan, 1962.

M.V. Alpatov, *Theophanes the Greek* (in Russian), Iskusstvo, Moscow, 1979.

V.N. Lazarev, *Russian Iconography* (in Russian), Iskusstvo, Moscow, 1983.

David Talbot Rice, *Kunst aus Byzanz,* Hirmer Verlag, Munich, 1959.

G.I. Vzdornov, *Theophanes the Greek* (in Russian), Iskusstvo, Moscow, 1983.

Liturgical texts

E. Mercenier, *La prière des Eglises de rite byzantin,* Ed. Chèvetogne, 1948.

Denis Guillaume, complete French translation of the Byzantine liturgical texts, Diaconie Apostolique, Rome, 1985.

The Festal Menaion and *The Lenten Triodion,* Faber and Faber, London-Boston.

Table of Illustrations

The illustrations in this book were generously made available by the Russian Ecumenical Center in Rome, Vicolo del Farinone, 30, Tel. 689-6637. For Figure 21 thanks are due to the Icon Museum of Recklinghausen.

9. *Virgin Hodigitria*
   School of Cyprus
   Beginning of the XIII century
   Church of St. Mary, Abbey of St. Nilus, Grottaferrata (Rome)

10. *The Virgin of Tenderness of Vladimir*
    Brought from Constantinople
    Beginning of the XII century, 100 × 70
    Tretiakov Gallery, Moscow

11. *The Belozersk Virgin of Tenderness*
    School of Novgorod
    XIII century, 156 × 107
    Russian Museum, Leningrad

12. *The Igorevsk Virgin of Tenderness*
    School of Novgorod
    End of XV-Beginning of XVI century, 69 × 48
    Russian Museum, Leningrad

13. *The Yaroslavl Virgin of Tenderness*
    School of Moscow
    Second half of XV century, 54 × 42
    Tretiakov Gallery, Moscow

14. The *Order of the Deësis*
    School of Novgorod
    XV century, central panel 157 × 108;
    other panels 160 × 59
    Tretiakov Gallery, Moscow

15. *The Virgin (Deësis)*
    Theophanes the Greek
    c. 1405, 210 × 110
    Cathedral of the Annunciation
    The Kremlin, Moscow

16. *St. John the Baptist (Deësis)*
    Disciple of Andrei Rublev
    First half of XV century, 104 × 84 (cut off in the XVII century)
    Andrei Rublev Museum, Moscow

17. *The Apostle Paul (Deësis of Zvenigorod)*
Andrei Rublev
1410-1420, 158 × 106
Tretiakov Gallery, Moscow

18. *The Archangel Michael (Deësis of Zvenigorod)*
Andrei Rublev
1410-1420, 158 × 108
Tretiakov Gallery, Moscow

19. *St. George*
School of Novgorod
End of XV century, 59 × 42
Russian Museum, Leningrad

20. *The Twelve Feasts of the Church*
Russian Icon
XVII century
Private collection

21. *The Conception of St. Anne*
School of Novgorod
XV century, 32 × 37
Recklinghausen Museum

22. *The Annunciation*
School of Novgorod
End of XII century, 238 × 169
Tretiakov Gallery, Moscow

23. *The Nativity*
School of A. Rublev
Beginning of XV century, 71 × 54
Tretiakov Gallery, Moscow

24. *The Baptism*
Greek School
XIV century, 51 × 37
Greek Patriarchate

25. *The Transfiguration* (order of the Feasts from the Church of Volotovo)
School of Novgorod
Last quarter of XV century, 90 × 58
Museum of History and Architecture, Novgorod

26. *The Last Supper*
    The School of Novgorod
    XV century, 90 × 63
    State Museum of Art, Kiev

27. *The Crucifixion*
    School of Moscow
    End of XIV century, 107 × 83
    Rublev Museum, Moscow

28. *The Descent into Hell* (order of the Feasts from the Church of Volotovo)
    School of Novgorod
    Last quarter of XVX century, 90 × 56
    Museum of History and Architecture, Novgorod

29. *The Ascension*
    Disciple of Andrei Rublev
    c. 1410-1420, 71 × 59
    Tretiakov Gallery, Moscow

30. *The Descent of the Holy Spirit* (Pentecost)
    School of Novgorod
    XV century, 80 × 56

31. *The Dormition*
    School of Tver'
    Middle of XV century, 133 × 88
    Tretiakov Gallery, Moscow

32. *The Trinity*
    Andrei Rublev
    Cathedral of the Trinity of St. Sergius
    c. 1411, 142 × 114
    Tretiakov Gallery, Moscow

Abbreviations Used in Citations
from Sacred Scripture
(in alphabetical order)

Ac	=	Acts of the Apostles
1 Co	=	1 Corinthians
2 Co	=	2 Corinthians
Col	=	Colossians
Dn	=	Daniel
Ep	=	Ephesians
Ex	=	Exodus
Ezk	=	Ezekiel
Ga	=	Galatians
Gn	=	Genesis
Heb	=	Hebrews
Ho	=	Hosea
Is	=	Isaiah
Jn	=	John
1 Jn	=	1 John
Lk	=	Luke
2 M	=	2 Maccabees
Mk	=	Mark
Mt	=	Matthew
1 P	=	1 Peter
Ph	=	Philippians
Ps	=	Psalms
Rv	=	Revelation
Rm	=	Romans
Sg	=	Song of Solomon
PG	=	*Patrologia Graeca*

SP **St. Paul Book & Media Centers:**

Alexandria, VA
Anchorage, AK
Boston, MA
Charleston, SC
Chicago, IL
Cleveland, OH
Dedham, MA
Edison, NJ
Honolulu, HI
Los Angeles, CA
Miami, FL
New Orleans, LA
New York, NY
King of Prussia, PA
San Antonio, TX
San Diego, CA
San Francisco, CA
St. Louis, MO
Staten Island, NY
Toronto, Ontario, CANADA